# AMPLE HILLS

## CREAMERY

# AMPLE HILLS CREAMERY

secrets & stories from Brooklyn's Favorite ICE CREAM SHOP

BRIAN SMITH
JACKIE CUSCUNA
• with •
LAUREN KAELIN

illustrated by
LAUREN KAELIN

photography by
LUCY SCHAEFFER

Abrams, New York

# CONTENTS

FOREWORD

# A SPOON IN THE ROAD

IN OCTOBER 2010, just six days before my wife, Jackie, and I were scheduled to sign the lease for our first ice cream shop here in Brooklyn, I got a phone call from God. Well, it felt like God at the time.

It was a job offer from a major book publisher in New York. They wanted me to come in and oversee production of their audiobook line. You see, for eight years I'd been making a living (on and off, that is, and recently mostly off) producing and directing audiobooks, as well as writing the occasional half-man, half-gator monster movie. The last two years had been tough. Freelance work had dried up. The monsters weren't paying the bills. I was living off our nest egg, slowly eating away at it, while dreaming, planning to open Ample Hills Creamery. I loved ice cream. I loved the idea of opening a neighborhood shop, like something out of Sesame Street. But the risk—the pressure to succeed—was tremendous. Jackie and I have two little kids. She's a public school teacher. We were about to sink our life savings into an ice cream dream. I had zero experience running a business, no culinary background, and not one good reason to believe we could be successful. And here was a call from on high, offering me an escape hatch, if you will. A "real job," with security, health insurance, and sick days! If ever there was a fork in the road, this was it.

I feared Jackie secretly hoped that I'd take the job and save the family from my fantasies of an ice cream kingdom, but she didn't utter a word. To her credit, she said the decision was mine to make.

The problem was, I didn't feel like I had a choice. I told myself that Ample Hills could wait. I had two kids. I had to be responsible. I had to be able to provide for them. Before the phone call, the shop felt like my only chance at a job. I had an unwavering passion for Ample Hills, and ice cream, and I knew in my heart that I could make it work. But realistically, I was spending our nest egg to buy myself a job. Now that I had a choice, how in good conscience could I turn down the security of a *real* job? If I were single, with no kids, OK. But I wasn't. I decided to take the job.

Then Jackie spoke up. I'd been counting on her to be thrilled with my decision. Or at least relieved. But she wasn't. "If we open the shop, maybe we'll

9

struggle, maybe we'll just squeak by, maybe the kids won't have as much stuff," she said, "but they'll have a happy dad." She added, "I can't live with you if you're miserable, always asking, 'What if, what if?' Maybe taking the job's the responsible decision, but it's also the easier one, and is that what we want to teach the kids?" That was it, really. Ice cream makes people happy. Ice cream makes *me* happy.

In the years before we opened Ample Hills, I made ice cream for friends and family in the Adirondacks, on the porch of a log cabin overlooking a small wooded lake. Jackie and her family have summered there since she was a little girl. For the same three weeks, for over thirty years, the same families have rented the same cabins, and the children—and now their children—have grown up together. I am a late addition to the genealogy. I married into the Adirondack tribe, but I arrived with my old-fashioned hand-crank ice cream maker in tow, and they welcomed me. We'd gather on the porch, taking turns cranking, as we prepared gallons and gallons of ice cream for large ice cream socials. It was there that I developed most of the recipes in this book, dreaming up ideas, adjusting them here and there, collaborating with others, always asking for feedback. On that porch, with the encouragement and love of those friends and families, Ample Hills was born.

I always set out to make the best ice cream I'd ever had. Why aspire to make the second best, right? But I realized that what was even more fun than eating the ice cream was the communal experience of friends and family taking turns cranking away at that wooden contraption, the shared joy of opening up the canister and seeing those billowy ribbons of fresh ice cream. Jackie and I wanted to make Ample Hills a gathering place. A place where people would want to come to pass the time, to share an ice cream cone with their kids or a banana split with their girlfriend or boyfriend—or an ice cream cake at a birthday party.

Needless to say, I turned down that job offer.

Today you may find me climbing up from the basement, struggling to carry the twelfth bucket of base for the day. Or running back to the basement when the breaker trips and all the machines go silent. Or arguing with a vendor on the phone, furious that we didn't get a delivery of pistachios. Or yelling at the freezers, or sweet-talking them, or coaxing them through another heat wave. Or staggering home, my shirt splattered, tripping over my own feet at the end of a long day. But don't let any of that fool you. There's a better sleep waiting. I'm happier now. Our two little kids, Nonna Kai and Kaleo, never understood what it meant to have their daddy be a grumpy audiobook producer. But they sure know what it means to have him be a happy ice cream warrior.

It's been a few years since we opened Ample Hills. I've churned tens of thousands of gallons of ice cream. Made hundreds of flavors. Met countless wonderful families in our shop here in Brooklyn. And now I have this opportunity to share some of these stories, some of these recipes with you. As well as a few tips on how to sell your killer half-shark, half-elephant movie to Hollywood (OK, maybe I can't help with that).

But believe it or not, creating a movie monster isn't so different from creating a great flavor of ice cream. Really. If you're interested in monsters, you watch every monster movie you can get your hands on (preferably while eating pints of ice cream). You research mythical creatures—the Hydra, the Gryphon, the Cyclops. You write down sordid, terrifying details from your nightmares. You look up drawings of prehistoric beasts—the Megaladon, the Terror Bird, the Spinosaurus. You borrow the head of one, the tail of another . . . You play around with it until it belongs to you and hopefully feels somewhat fresh and new.

If you're interested in ice cream, you eat any and all ice cream you can get your hands on (preferably while watching old sci-fi and monster movies). You read ice cream cookbooks, cookie cookbooks, cake cookbooks. You walk up and down the aisles of the grocery store, studying ingredients. You borrow peanut butter from this flavor, honey-bacon cornbread from that one. You experiment. You play around with it until it belongs to you, and hopefully tastes somewhat fresh and new.

When you create a new flavor of ice cream, when you start a new screenplay, or do anything in the arts, you draw on your life experience . . . all the way back to childhood. Often, when I'm making new flavors, I'm aware of an innate desire to transport myself through cooking, through ice cream back in time . . . to make that connection to the kid I used to be. So I can experience a little of the wonder, the awe of first times again.

At seven, I was a strange kid. I listened to old-time radio shows like *The Shadow*, *X Minus One*, and *Fibber McGee and Molly*. My favorite movie star was Humphrey Bogart. I dreamed of going back in time to be a soda jerk at an ice cream parlor, while writing episodes of *The Shadow* at night and directing films alongside Orson Welles and John Huston on weekends. My dad had to break it to me that no one made radio drama anymore, there weren't soda jerks at ice cream shops, and Orson Welles and John Huston were dead. Oh, and time travel wasn't possible.

I spent the better part of my twenties trying to prove Dad wrong. Not about the time travel. He's still right about that. But I was able to make a go at revitalizing radio drama for a short while. During the first heyday of the dotcoms, I convinced Syfy channel to let me produce new audio dramas to be streamed online. I called it *Seeing Ear Theatre*, and it was wonderful. This was before video on the web, and much like television killed old-time radio drama in the United States, high-speed internet killed *Seeing Ear Theatre*.

After *Seeing Ear Theatre* died, and after I tried my hand at audiobook production, I decided to be a screenwriter. I'd always fantasized about the writing life, sitting alone in a secluded cabin deep in the woods, with a bottle of Jack Daniel's, tapping away at my antique typewriter. I took some screenwriting classes. I read every how-to book there was. And then I set up a writing office. I bought a gorgeous midcentury modern desk and hung up movie posters of *Brazil* and *The Wicker Man* for inspiration. I bought a 1905 Underwood No. 5 typewriter, and I set to work.

I had some limited success, selling a couple of TV movies to Syfy channel. In one of them, aliens board a runaway train. In another, giant killer birds threaten the eastern seaboard. In yet another, a group of kids on a rowboat battle a hideous half-otter, half-fish monster. The problem is, that secluded cabin deep in the woods is really, really lonely. And writing is brutal. For me to gather the courage to commit words to paper, I had to believe that they were the best words ever written—such euphoria! But of course they weren't—such despair. I ate pints of Ben & Jerry's ice cream (my Jack Daniel's) and began to fantasize about opening an ice cream parlor. Where people would gather, where friends and family would always be close by . . . where everyone would know my name.

I didn't have the disposition to be a full-time writer. It was a hard truth to come by, but I learned that I preferred having written to actually writing. I loved sorting all those crisp three-holed pages; I loved fastening those shiny brass tabs, running my hand along the 108-page spine of my script. But the writing life just wasn't for me, and the proof is in my waistline. Since opening the shop in May 2011, I've lost twenty-five pounds. Sitting and writing for twelve hours a day created such anxiety, such agita, that I could easily down a pint of ice cream a day. Now, though I eat ice cream for breakfast, lunch, and dinner, I'm only tasting it. And I'm on my feet all day long, running tubs of ice cream up and down the steps to the freezers.

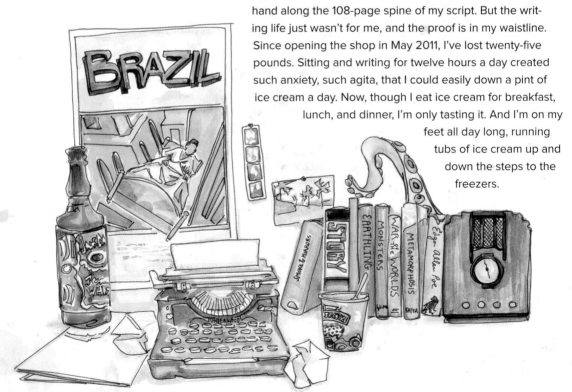

And fans of Syfy channel are better off, too. There are better writers and scarier monsters out there chomping at the legs of innocent teenagers. I'll stick to Brain Freeze (our zombie-inspired flavor, with gummy brains and swirls of strawberry blood). Now I pour my Jack Daniel's into the ice cream maker for our Bourbon St. flavor (page 117). Okay, it's Maker's Mark, actually—this is an artisanal ice cream shop, after all.

And so here we are: The *Ample Hills Creamery* cookbook is in your hands. What a strange, joyous trip to have come full circle, back to writing. Yes, it's still as difficult as ever, and yet it's somehow even more rewarding to run my hands along the spine of this book. Maybe that's because this book is a collaboration. Not just between myself and my co-authors. But with you. This book is about helping you make the best ice cream you've ever had. But for that to happen, you have to meet us halfway. You've got to bring something of yourself, some of your creativity and monster-making genius to the process.

In the pages that follow, we share the groundwork and give you the recipes for some of our most popular flavors, but really our hope is that you don't follow the instructions line for line. Take pieces from one recipe and combine them with pieces from another. Make something new. Do it with your friends or family.

If you have good ingredients and you start with the right ratio of milk to cream to sugar, it's really hard to create inedible ice cream. But go ahead and try. That's half the fun.

Then come and find me at the shop on Vanderbilt, and bring me some!

—BRIAN SMITH

# NEW YORK, BORN AND RAISED

I WANTED OUR FAMILY TO BE HAPPY. I wanted Brian to actualize his ice cream–making dream and I wanted our kids to be in the presence of happy parents fully enjoying their lives and both of their children. I also wanted to create a community gathering spot.

I was born and raised in New York City, and I'm proud to be a New Yorker for many reasons. Living in this city has given me many gifts that I cherish deeply. One gift is the way in which I've always been able to find community. People are everywhere in New York. We are stacked on top of each other in buildings and pressed up against each other in buses. We walk in large masses across busy streets. We are attracted to places where there are lots of people and long waits. And communities seem to spring up in the most unexpected places: in the subway or while waiting on line for coffee. Communities collect easily and while some are sustained, others are fleeting. A subway car erupts into song. A street corner becomes a political debate. The coffee line becomes a klatch. A park transforms into an after-hours club.

I have always loved to travel but somehow have never had the desire to leave my home base. When I'd arrive back in New York after a long journey, a sense of calm and relief would come over me as I'd interact with my people, my crazily diverse city brethren. I love everything about living here. I love the ability to get around town on public transportation. I love the many different neighborhoods spanning the five boroughs and the cultural variety they offer. I love the museums, the parks, the free events, the water, the nighttime, the lights, the food. Mmm, yes, the food—there's so much out there—and whenever a craving hits, there's usually a way to sate it at almost any hour of the day or night. More than anything, I love the people. Where there are people, there is energy. Energy that can be ecstatic, frenzied, rhapsodic, mellow, loving, and, most of all, spirited and contagious. It is this contagious spirit of life that fuels my love of New York.

I grew up in New York in the seventies and eighties, and I have vivid childhood memories of ice cream shops. I remember going to Eddie's with my grandmother, sitting in one of the long wooden booths, ordering a banana split with strawberry ice cream (her favorite), and watching the overflowing, perfectly oval mound of whipped cream make its way up from the basement. I remember attending a friend's tenth birthday party at Jahn's Ice Cream Parlor in Richmond Hill. We danced to Michael Jackson's newly released single "Rock with You" and shared Jahn's infamous Kitchen Sink mega-sundae. I remember my dad taking me to Serendipity after attending acting class a few blocks away, then going there a few years later—when I could ride the subway by myself—and meeting my friends for a "grown-up" outing. And I remember stopping with my family at The Lemon Ice King of Corona on the way home from Jones Beach to get a pint of cherry ice to go, served in a Chinese-food takeout container.

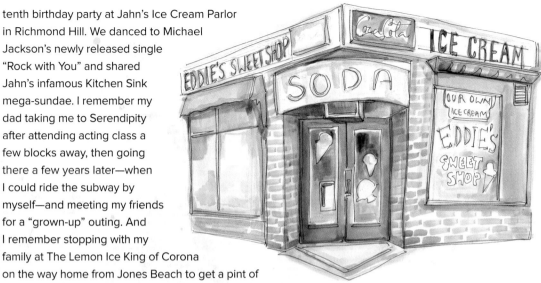

Each of these memories sparks deeper connections that link me to flavors, sensations, feelings, and places that other kindred New Yorkers have experienced. It's this interconnectedness of people over time that Walt Whitman speaks of in "Crossing Brooklyn Ferry," and it's what Brian and I wished to impart to our community with the creation of Ample Hills. All of our memories have a connectedness to other people, some we know but millions we don't, and it is through these shared senses, feelings, and experiences that we become humanity. Walt Whitman said:

> The similitudes of the past, and those of the future;
> The glories strung like beads on my smallest sights and hearings—on the walk in the street, and the passage over the river . . .
> The others that are to follow me, the ties between me and them . . .
> What is it, then, between us?
> What is the count of the scores or hundreds of years between us?
> Whatever it is, it avails not—distance avails not, and place avails not.
> I too lived—Brooklyn, of Ample Hills, was mine . . .

This is what Brian and I want to share with our children, Nonna Kai and Kaleo, and to New York—a place where community happens. A place that might, for whatever reason, become etched in the heart and written in the memory of another little girl sitting with her grandma or her friends or her dad, and years from now she will say, "When I was a kid, there was an ice cream shop in Brooklyn . . . "

—JACKIE CUSCUNA

# THE SECRET TO MAKING GREAT ICE CREAM

ACTUALLY, THERE'S NO SECRET TO MAKING GREAT ICE CREAM. **Not really. At** its most pure, ice cream is just frozen milk, cream, sugar, and eggs. What separates great ice cream from mediocre ice cream is the quality of those ingredients—and the process by which they're prepared and churned into a frozen product.

Master our sweet cream base (Walt's Dream, page 24), and then open your pantry or scour the aisles of the grocery store, and have some fun!

# INGREDIENTS

## SKIM MILK POWDER

**OK, there is one *kinda* secret ingredient.** It's something that nearly all commercial ice cream makers use. That's skim milk powder, or nonfat dry milk powder. Sounds fancy, but really it's just dehydrated milk. Ice cream makers use it to combat the effects of too much water in their ice cream base. Milk is almost 90 percent water, and heavy cream is about 60 percent water. You need water to freeze your ice cream, but too much water will freeze into itty-bitty ice crystals . . . and your ice cream will be icy and grainy, not smooth and creamy. Skim milk powder absorbs excess water and gives a milkier, creamier flavor.

Most home ice cream recipes call for a two-to-one (or higher!) ratio of heavy cream to milk. That's a lot of extra cream. The reason for this is that cream has more butterfat, more body, and less water in it than milk does, and the recipes are attempting to compensate for the high water content of milk. Our recipes generally call for a one-to-one ratio of cream to milk. Skim milk powder allows us to do this, absorbing excess water and creating a smooth, creamy finished product. And one that's less heavy and fattening.

## ORGANIC CANE SUGAR

Refined white sugar is boring. It's sweet, yes. And it'll get the job done. But nearly all of the natural flavors from the original sugarcane plant have been processed away. We recommend using organic cane sugar, which hasn't been refined to the same extent. It's more expensive but worth every cent. Yellow-brown in color, organic cane sugar has subtle notes of molasses and caramel. And unlike refined white sugar, it retains actual nutrients from the sugarcane plant.

## LYLE'S GOLDEN SYRUP

Bakers, candy makers, and ice cream makers use corn syrup for textural reasons. Corn syrup is an invert sugar, and, as such, it helps prevent sugar crystals from forming, keeping confections smooth and glossy. The problem is that corn syrup, just like white sugar, is boring. It's a supersweet sugar processed from corn. But it doesn't have much flavor.

When we need a liquid sugar, we usually opt for Lyle's Golden Syrup. It's more expensive than corn syrup, but worth it! It's made from sugarcane, and has strong notes of toffee and caramel. It adds a rich, almost nutty complexity to many of our brittles, and it's the secret weapon in our intoxicating hot fudge.

## MILK AND CREAM

We recommend seeking out pasteurized milk and cream, as opposed to the more easily accessible ultra-pasteurized dairy products. Ultra-pasteurization involves heating milk or cream to a much higher temperature (280°F/140°C, as opposed to 165°F/75°C for pasteurization). This prolongs shelf life, but sacrifices quality and taste. It's like a well-done steak compared to a medium-rare one.

Pasteurized milk (versus ultra-pasteurized) might not be available at your local grocery store, but specialty grocery stores should have it. It's worth the search; you can taste the difference.

## BUTTER

You'll want to use European-style butter, which has a higher fat content (83 to 86 percent butterfat) than conventional American butter (81 to 82 percent butterfat). Fat carries flavor, so your cookies and brownies will be richer and have more pop. Choose unsalted butter, as this will allow you to control the amount of salt you use in your recipes.

## EGGS

We support small farms that raise their chickens humanely. Of course, it's the right thing to do—but it's not all about altruism. Happier chickens produce better-tasting eggs, pure and simple. Seek out large fresh, organic, cage-free, or free-range eggs if you can.

## EXTRACTS AND FOOD COLORINGS

At Ample Hills, we only use all-natural extracts. Even our cotton candy extract is all-natural (sourced from Nature's Flavors). We try not to put anything into our ice cream that we can't pronounce! But really, no artificial flavor can

stand up to the quality of the real thing. Use 100 percent pure vanilla, pure peppermint, and the like, and it'll make a big difference.

When you want to color your ice cream blue or green or red, we recommend using all-natural food dyes. They are trickier to use than artificial colorings because all-natural dyes come from vegetable and plant sources and often impart flavor when used in large doses. So experiment. It's rewarding to create a colorful, fun recipe using all-natural ingredients—but we won't judge you if you break down and use artificial colors. We've had to do it from time to time!

## EQUIPMENT CHECKLIST

- Ice cream maker
- 1-quart (960-ml) storage containers
- 12-by-18-inch (30-by-46-inch) rimmed baking sheet
- 2-quart (2-L) saucepan
- Candy thermometer *
- Food processor (optional)
- Heatproof mixing bowl
- Heatproof spatula
- Blender or immersion blender (recommended)
- Scale
- Whisk
- Wire-mesh strainer and cheesecloth

* A CANDY THERMOMETER is recommended to measure the temperature of the ice cream base when you're heating it on your stovetop. Most ice cream cookbooks instruct cooks to guesstimate the correct temperature as the point at which the base "coats the back of a wooden spoon." It's much easier—and much more precise—to just use a candy thermometer. Be sure to swirl the thermometer throughout the mixture in order to get a more accurate reading.

# HAND CRANK, THE OLD-FASHIONED WAY

Most readily accessible ice cream makers today include a gel insert that you put in the freezer overnight before pouring in the base and churning. We recommend using an old-fashioned hand-crank ice cream maker, which uses rock salt and ice to freeze the mixture. Rock salt rapidly drops the freezing temperature of ice and, in effect, makes a very, very cold slush that surrounds and freezes the ice cream. This slush reaches colder temperatures (and does so more quickly) than any gel freezer on the market. And the faster and colder you freeze your ice cream, the smoother and creamier it will be. This is because there'll be less time for ice crystals to grow.

Hand-crank machines are messier, for sure. Water and salt end up all over the counter and floor. But they're also a lot more fun to use. There's a sense of community that forms around making ice cream, with friends and family taking turns cranking, adding more ice and salt, and telling stories. You feel a connection through time, to your parents and grandparents, and their parents, who made ice cream just the same way—fifty, a hundred, a hundred and fifty years ago. Your clothes may be different, and your music, and your mode of transportation. Buildings around you may have come and gone. But the method of making ice cream hasn't budged. Use a hand-crank ice cream maker, and you'll experience a deeper appreciation and respect for the finished product. Country Freezer (www.country-freezer.com) makes beautiful, high-quality hand-crank machines.

## THE FIRST HAND-CRANK ICE CREAM MAKER

In 1843, Nancy Johnson invented the hand-crank ice cream maker. Until then, people made ice cream by the French pot method, mixing milk, cream, sugar, and eggs in nested bowls—one bowl set in another bowl filled with ice and salt. This method took longer and required constantly stirring the mixture as it slowly froze. Nancy Johnson's invention enclosed the mixture in a metal cylinder, keeping it colder, freezing it faster, and using a dasher blade to churn the ice cream. This dasher blade adds another ingredient as it spins around: air! Air gives ice cream lift and body, making it poofy and smooth, like a cloud.

# ABOUT THIS BOOK

THE CHAPTERS IN THE PAGES THAT FOLLOW feature flavors that have been made famous at our shop in Brooklyn. While most ice cream cookbooks divide their flavors seasonally—pineapples and strawberries in the summertime, apples in the fall, and chocolate in the winter—at Ample Hills, we like eating chocolate in spring, too, and apples in summer, and yes, even pineapples in the winter. It all depends on what mood we're in.

At Ample Hills, there's ice cream for any occasion. There's an ice cream for when you're tearfully watching *When Harry Met Sally*. Or when you have the late-night epiphany that potato chips, pretzels, and ice cream would taste *really* good together. There's an ice cream for when you miss your grandmother's cookies, for when you need a drink, for when you want to celebrate. And yes, there's also good old-fashioned strawberry ice cream.

When we started to organize the flavors for this cookbook, we decided to pay homage to these relationships and arrange the flavors by mood. So, whether you are feeling a little crazy, creative, tired, sad, or anything else under the sun, it's easy to find exactly the kind of ice cream you feel like making (and eating!).

# GETTING STARTED

Most of the recipes in this book begin with a sweet cream base we call Walt's Dream (page 24). We recommend perfecting this simple recipe first before moving on to the more elaborate pretzel-, popcorn-, or marshmallow-infused ones. In addition, there are a few basic techniques that you'll need to master.

## STEEPING

This is one of the key techniques for imparting flavor to ice cream. Steeping ingredients, or soaking them in the base used to make the ice cream, opens up a whole new world of flavor possibilities. You aren't limited to a vanilla or chocolate base—you can make rye bread–infused ice cream, popcorn-infused ice cream, or even Cheetos-infused ice cream.

The key to steeping is to heat the milk first, until it starts to steam. Then remove the pan from the heat, add the ingredient to be steeped, and cover the pan with a tight-fitting lid. Let sit at least 20 minutes. Stir occasionally. The longer you steep, the more concentrated the flavor will become. Our recipes specify the recommended steeping time, which varies according to ingredient and the desired intensity of the flavor.

## TEMPERING EGG YOLKS

Tempering egg yolks is an important technique for creating the right creamy consistency in ice cream. You don't want to dump raw egg yolks into a pot of hundred-plus-degree milk, cream, and sugar, because the yolks will cook and form clumps. Start with your egg yolks in a medium bowl and your milk mixture heating on the stove. When the milk mixture reaches 100°F to 110°F (40°C to 45°C), remove the mixture from the heat. Ladle out about ½ cup (120 ml) and, while whisking, slowly pour this into the egg yolks to temper them. Once the egg-yolk mixture is an even color and consistency, whisk it back into the pan with the remaining milk mixture and continue to gradually heat it. Just in case any clumps have formed, we recommend straining your mix through a wire-mesh strainer before churning.

## ICE BATH

We cook (or pasteurize) our ice cream base in order to kill as many microorganisms as possible, making the ice cream safe to eat. But if we don't cool our cooked base quickly—if we take the 165°F (75°C) base and stick it in the refrigerator, for example—the time it takes for the temperature to fall back to 40°F to 45°F (5°C to 10°C) allows for those microorganisms to multiply again. That's why we use an ice bath to rapidly cool the base.

The easiest place to create an ice bath is in your kitchen sink. Fill the sink a quarter of the way with cold water and add a few handfuls of ice. Then gently lower the ice cream base into the ice bath. Let cool for 15 to 20 minutes, stirring occasionally. Make sure your base has cooled completely before churning.

## ADDING SWIRLS AND MIX-INS

Nearly all swirls and mix-ins are added after the ice cream has been churned. Otherwise, swirls would simply blend into the ice cream as it churns, and mix-ins would sink to the bottom. When the ice cream has finished churning, get a freezer-proof plastic storage container. This is the time to add swirls and mix-ins. For swirls, transfer two scoops of ice cream to the storage container, then drizzle (or spoon) the chocolate (or jam or peanut butter) over the ice cream. Be careful not to overmix it into the ice cream. Repeat with two more scoops of ice cream, more drizzle, and so on, until all of the ice cream has been added to the storage container and mixed with the swirl. Move quickly or the ice cream will melt. Mix-ins are easier. Just stir them in as you transfer the ice cream to the storage container. Use as little or as much as you'd like. Our goal in the shop is to go overboard with mix-ins, but perhaps you prefer a lighter hand. It's up to you. All the recipes for mix-ins make approximately one tray, but that it is more than necessary for the recipe of ice cream. Enjoy the leftovers!

# FACTS AND FIGURES

- All of the recipes yield approximately **1 quart (960 ml) of ice cream**.
- One quart of ice cream should serve about **8 people**, or make **8 half-cup (120-ml) servings.**
- All of the recipes will keep for up to **1 week** (or so). After about a week, homemade ice cream will begin to form ice crystals and will lose its creamy, smooth texture.
- The recipes take **30 minutes or more** to complete.
- In a hand-crank ice cream maker, it should take about **30 minutes** to churn Walt's Dream.
- Make sure the mix is **completely cool** before churning.
- If you prefer super-creamy, soft-serve-style ice cream, feel free to serve it directly from your ice cream maker. If you want your ice cream to be more solid and scoopable—and you have some patience—we recommend freezing overnight, or until the ice cream is completely solid, which will take **8 to 12 hours**.

# HOW WE MAKE ICE CREAM AT AMPLE HILLS

BLAST FREEZER

BATCH FREEZER

OVEN

VAT PASTEURIZER

CHILLER

SINK

MIXER

only 175 square feet

Ice cream making isn't a quick process. At our shop, it takes us 2 days to make a full batch of ice cream. On Day 1, we run the VAT pasteurizer, cooking our blend of milk, cream, sugar, eggs, and skim milk powder. This takes about 5 hours. Then we cool our mix to 60 degrees in the 100-gallon chiller before moving the mix to the walk-in fridge, where it cools overnight even more (to 40 degrees). On Day 1 we also cook and chop our various mix-ins—brownies, cookies, etc. On Day 2, we churn the base into various flavors of ice cream. Churning each 6-gallon batch takes about 15 minutes. Then we harden the ice cream in our blast freezer for 8 to 12 hours.

# WALT'S DREAM

### pure sweet cream ice cream

**3/4 cup (150 g) organic cane sugar**

**1/2 cup (60 g) skim milk powder**

**1⅔ cups (400 ml) whole milk**

**1⅔ cups (400 ml) heavy cream**

**3 egg yolks**

1. Prepare an ice bath (see page 21) in your sink or in a large heatproof bowl.

2. In a medium saucepan, combine the sugar, skim milk powder, and milk. Stir with a hand mixer or whisk until smooth. Make sure the skim milk powder is wholly dissolved into the mixture and that no lumps remain (any remaining sugar granules will dissolve over the heat). Stir in the cream.

3. Clip a candy thermometer to the saucepan and set the pan over medium heat. Cook, stirring often with a rubber spatula and scraping the bottom of the pan to prevent sticking and burning, until the mixture reaches 110°F (45°C), 5 to 10 minutes. Remove the pan from the heat.

4. Place the egg yolks in a medium bowl. While whisking, slowly pour in ½ cup (120 ml) of the hot milk mixture to temper the egg yolks. Continue to whisk slowly until the mixture is an even color and

consistency, then whisk the egg-yolk mixture back into the remaining milk mixture.

5. Return the pan to the stovetop over medium heat and continue cooking the mixture, stirring often, until it reaches 165°F (75°C), 5 to 10 minutes more.

6. Transfer the pan to the prepared ice bath and let cool for 15 to 20 minutes, stirring occasionally. Pour the ice cream base through a wire-mesh strainer into a storage container and place in the refrigerator for 1 to 2 hours, or until completely cool.

7. Now you're ready to make ice cream! Transfer the cooled base to an ice cream maker and churn it according to the manufacturer's instructions. Or, if you want, you can keep it in the refrigerator for up to 3 days before churning.

8. After churning, serve immediately or harden in your freezer for 8 to 12 hours for a more scoopable ice cream.

# KIDS IN THE KITCHEN

As serious as we are about our craft at Ample Hills, we never forget why we make ice cream. For the kids. For your kids, for our kids—and for the kids inside all of us.

Our first scoop. Our first cone. Our first sundae. Perhaps it's these memories we're in search of when we dig into a pint of ice cream as adults, trying to reconnect to the children we used to be.

When we started brainstorming ways to make this cookbook echo that philosophy, we wanted to rework the antiquated Mommy-and-Me approach. How can our kids, and your kids, be involved in the kitchen without being in the way? How can we help them make memories that they'll hold on to throughout their lives? Making ice cream, toffees, and swirls is pretty complicated and can sometimes be very dangerous. Little hands have no place near molten sugar! So we have highlighted kid-friendly tasks and activities that can engage the little ones in making the recipe (and keep them at a safe distance from the stove).

Outside of the kitchen and away from hot caramel, encourage your kids to open this cookbook. We've added elements specifically for them—activities, hidden goblets, chubby chickens, and an adventure story. But don't be put off by these—they are intended for you, too. You should play, search, and read as well; after all, who isn't a kid when it comes to ice cream?

# OUR FIRST FOUR DAYS

Ample Hills first became known as the ice cream shop so popular we sold out of all our ice cream in just four days. Whether it was poor planning, good luck, or the best problem we could have had, those first four days shaped Ample Hills into the business it is today.

### DAY 1: MAY 25, 2011

We had no prior experience running a business and no idea what to expect. Opening day was both thrilling and terrifying. Our creation was about to be presented to the world. Would people like us? Would they come back? People were tasting and smiling and complimenting our ice cream. Back home, after an exhilarating first day, we sunk into our bed exhausted. It was much like the first night home with our newborn daughter, Nonna, in bed between us as we thought: *What have we done? Where do we go from here?*

### DAYS 2 & 3: MAY 26 & 27

Lines of people held steady for the next two days. Our excitement began to turn into anxiety as we realized we would soon run out of ice cream. We could not produce enough ice cream at the rate we were selling it. We hadn't planned for success. By Days 2 and 3 it was clear that there was a desire for our homemade, homespun ice cream—and now we feared we couldn't meet that demand.

### DAY 4: MAY 28

Salted Crack Caramel was the first flavor to go. Peppermint Pattie was a close second.

By the end of the night there was only one: Bubblegum. We scooped it until it was gone . . . We closed our doors an hour early on a warm Saturday evening on Memorial Day weekend, hoping to open soon.

### THE DAYS AFTER

We worked hard to reopen, stockpile ice cream, and create a system that would allow us to be successful and still stay in business. We got a lot of help from family, friends, employees, employees who became friends, and customers who became loyal employees. We reopened our doors with a larger staff and a full cabinet of ice cream. We have continued to attract happy people, an incredible staff, and good press—all of which contribute to the ongoing evolution of our little shop.

### SELL-OUT CELEBRATION

Each year, to celebrate our anniversary and honor our beginnings, our loyal customers, and our growing pains, we have a Sell-Out Celebration. We start the day with twenty-four full boxes of ice cream and sell out, decreasing the cost of each flavor until it's free!

# INTRODUCTIONS: WALT, WHITTY, AND PB

A cow seems a natural emblem for an ice cream parlor. As the producer of 80 to 90 percent of the ingredients in ice cream, it's only fitting that a fresh-faced cow is featured prominently in our logo. Gradually, however, this amorphous character started to develop his own fully formed personality: Walt, named after Walt Whitman. Walt the Cow would go on to make friends with Whitty the Chicken and Peanut Butter the Pig (PB, for short). There are also some seasonal cameos from Sprinkles the Penguin and Gobbles the Turkey.

Walt, Whitty, and PB have developed elaborate backstories, motivations, and personalities.

- **Walt** the cow is earnest, foolhardy, and maybe a little gullible. He has blue ears and loves naps.
- **Whitty** is a bit brash, but fiercely loyal. He is clunky and excitable, and likes to play dress up.
- **PB** is everyone's favorite. He loves ice cream, peanut butter, and not taking long walks.

# MEET THE AMPLOYEES

That's right, we are called Amployees, and each year we have an Ampleversary. And one day, we'll have Amplympics.

Brent · Vanessa · Jackie · Brian · Lauren A. · Eric · Lauren K. · Adam · Christian

The influence of all these key people can be seen throughout the pages to follow. But our friends Walt, Whitty, and PB will be your guides through the cookbook, by way of an adventure. First, they go on a picnic . . .

Dark Chocolate
(page 36)

Breakfast
Trash (page 68)

Salted Crack
Caramel
(page 146)

Peppermint
Pattie
(page 151)

Cotton Candy
(page 84)

Pistachio Squared
(page 103)

# BLISSFUL

for WHEN YOU
crave SomeTHing simple
YeT SuBLime

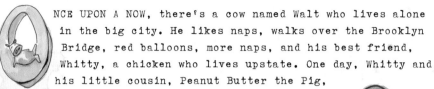NCE UPON A NOW, there's a cow named Walt who lives alone
in the big city. He likes naps, walks over the Brooklyn
Bridge, red balloons, more naps, and his best friend,
Whitty, a chicken who lives upstate. One day, Whitty and
his little cousin, Peanut Butter the Pig,
come to visit Walt. Their favorite thing to do
together is nothing. On a blanket in the park. Well,
Walt and Whitty like to do nothing, but PB likes
to eat ice cream. Ice cream for breakfast. And for
lunch. And for dinner. And for dessert, of course. And
at snack time. And at middle-of-the-morning mealtime.

"That's not a meal," says Whitty.

"Is too," says PB. And for PB it is.

Whitty watches the clouds billow and dance across the sky.
"Oooh, a shark! No, an elephant. With fins. Riding a bus.
Do you see it?" But Walt doesn't look. He is trying very hard
to take a nap.

And at that very moment, PB finishes his last bite of ice cream.
He does not pause to think about how wonderful it was. Instead he
says, "More, please." But as it happens with most picnics, there
isn't any more ice cream. PB cries and screams and oinks. Whitty
takes PB in his arms and starts telling him a story.

"Once upon a time, there lived a king and queen, and they had a
little girl who was always very sad. She wanted more."

"More what?" PB asks.

"More everything. More horses. More dresses
with polka dots. More oatmeal."

"Yuck." PB sticks his tongue out.

"More ice cream," Whitty corrects himself.

"Yummy."

"So the king summoned every court magician from far and wide, across
all the kingdoms in the land, and asked each one for a spell to
make the little princess happy. But none had such a powerful spell.
Finally, the last magician arrived. He offered no spell. Instead he

handed the king a simple purple goblet made of clay. 'This will make
the princess happy,' the magician declared. 'But it's just a dumb
bowl, Daddy,' the princess cried when he gave it to her. In it was
a heaping scoop of triple chocolate fudge ice
cream. 'And I don't even like purple.' But she
ate the ice cream, and it was good. When she
finished, she was sad. As she always was. But
then she looked down into her empty bowl and a
smile crossed her face. Her bowl wasn't empty.
There was another scoop of triple chocolate
fudge ice cream there, even bigger than the
last. She gobbled it up. And again, her bowl
wasn't empty. She ate and ate and ate, and
for the first time, she ate in total bliss,
always knowing that there would never be a
last bite."

"I want that bowl!" PB yells. "Let's find
the bowl! Is it buried somewhere? Do you know
where it is? Is it hidden in a castle, or in a
dragon's lair? Let's get it!"

Whitty explains to PB that it is just a story.

"That doesn't mean it's not true," PB says.

"That's exactly what it means. It's pretend. Walt, tell PB what
pretend means."

Walt sits up. "My mom told me the same story when I was a calf. I
thought it was make-believe, too, but now . . . after hearing the same
story from you, Whitty, I think it must be true."

Whitty jumps up and down, and clucks, "I just made it up! Just now!
Five minutes ago! I made it up! Your mom made it up!"

"Let's go and find it!" says PB.

"After a nap," says Walt. "Yes. After a nap."

# VANILLA BEAN

There's nothing boring or plain about real vanilla ice cream. Vanilla beans are exotic and beautiful, and oh so fragrant and flavorful. We steep the beans and add vanilla extract as well, for a double dose of vanilla perfection. In addition, we throw in a handful of coffee beans. They add a kick and a complexity to vanilla ice cream. Not enough to make it taste like coffee, but just enough to give you a hint of something nutty, bitter, and slightly beyond your reach.

1 vanilla bean

1 recipe Walt's Dream (page 24)

30 whole coffee beans

1½ teaspoons vanilla extract

1. Halve the vanilla bean lengthwise and gently scrape the seeds from inside the husks.

2. Prepare Walt's Dream according to the recipe directions, adding the vanilla bean pod and seeds and the coffee beans before heating the milk mixture.

3. Transfer the pan to the ice bath and let cool for 15 to 20 minutes. Pour the base through a wire-mesh strainer into a bowl to remove the coffee beans and vanilla bean pod. Stir in the vanilla extract. Place in the refrigerator for 1 to 2 hours, or until completely cooled.

4. Transfer the cooled base to an ice cream maker and churn it according to the manufacturer's instructions.

5. Transfer the ice cream to a storage container. Serve immediately or harden in your freezer for 8 to 12 hours for a more scoopable ice cream.

If you're feeling classical, pour hot fudge all over a scoop of vanilla bean and listen to some Bach.

# DARK CHOCOLATE

1 cup (200 g) organic cane sugar

1 cup (90 g) cocoa powder

4 ounces (115 g) semisweet or bittersweet chocolate, chopped

1 recipe Walt's Dream (page 24)

1 teaspoon vanilla extract

A young man came into the shop one afternoon in a rush and asked for four chocolate milk-shakes. He explained that his wife was about to go into labor and a dark-chocolate milk-shake was the only thing she wanted before her scheduled home birth. He figured he'd order four of them just to be safe.

We use Valrhona cocoa powder and E. Guittard 72 percent cacao chocolate for a rich, deep, dark chocolate ice cream. At the shop, we don't offer a regular mild chocolate ice cream. And surprisingly, this super-dark chocolate has become a favorite with our younger customers, too.

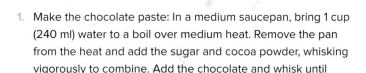

1. Make the chocolate paste: In a medium saucepan, bring 1 cup (240 ml) water to a boil over medium heat. Remove the pan from the heat and add the sugar and cocoa powder, whisking vigorously to combine. Add the chocolate and whisk until melted and combined. Set aside to cool.

2. Prepare Walt's Dream according to the recipe directions. Before you cool the base in the ice bath, stir in the chocolate paste and vanilla. Cool the mixture in the ice bath for 15 to 20 minutes. Pour the ice cream base through a wire-mesh strainer into a storage container and place in the refrigerator for 1 to 2 hours, or until completely cool.

3. Transfer the cooled base to an ice cream maker and churn it according to the manufacturer's instructions.

4. Transfer the ice cream to a storage container. Serve immediately or harden in your freezer for 8 to 12 hours for a more scoopable ice cream.

# RASPBERRY BLONDE

Butter for the baking sheet

1 cup plus 2 tablespoons (160 g) bread flour

1½ cups (185 g) all-purpose flour

1⅛ teaspoons salt

⅓ cup (40 g) malt powder

14 tablespoons (210 g) unsalted butter, at room temperature

1 tablespoon plus ½ teaspoon vegetable shortening

1¾ cups (385 g) packed dark brown sugar

3 eggs

2¼ teaspoons vanilla extract

7 ounces (200 g) white chocolate, chopped into small pieces

7 ounces (200 g) milk chocolate, chopped into small pieces

From the very beginning, Jackie (as well as everyone else who worked at the shop) pushed Brian to make fruit flavors. But besides orange juice, Brian never really liked fruit that much (or vegetables, for that matter). For a long time, this was the only "fruit" flavor at Ample Hills, even though it was really a white chocolate ice cream with swirls of raspberry jam. The malt blondies are rich with caramel notes; they stay chewy in the ice cream.

1. Make the malt blondies: Preheat the oven to 350°F (175°C). Lightly butter a 12-by-18-inch rimmed baking sheet and line it with parchment paper, pressing the parchment neatly into all four corners.

2. In a medium bowl, whisk together the bread flour, all-purpose flour, salt, and malt powder. Set aside.

3. In the bowl of a stand mixer fitted with the paddle attachment, beat together the butter, shortening, and brown sugar on medium speed until smooth. Add the eggs and vanilla and beat briefly to combine. Add the flour mixture and beat on low speed until just combined, being careful not to overmix. Fold in the white and milk chocolate pieces, and spread the mixture evenly over the prepared baking sheet. Bake for 25 minutes.

4. Cool the malt blondies completely, then chop them into bite-size pieces. Set aside.

5. Make the white chocolate ice cream: Prepare Walt's Dream according to the recipe directions. When the base reaches 165°F (75°C), remove the pan from the heat and add the white chocolate. Stir until the white chocolate melts. Transfer the pan to the ice bath and let cool for 15 to 20 minutes. Pour the ice cream base through a wire-mesh strainer into a storage container and place in the refrigerator for 1 to 2 hours, or until completely cool.

6. Transfer the cooled base to an ice cream maker and churn it according to the manufacturer's instructions.

7. Transfer the ice cream to a storage container, folding in the malt blondie pieces as you do. Use as many of the blondie pieces as you want; you won't necessarily need the whole batch. Then gently fold in heaping spoonfuls of the raspberry jam, softly lifting and spinning it throughout the ice cream. Be careful not to overmix. Serve immediately or harden in your freezer for 8 to 12 hours for a more scoopable ice cream.

FOR THE WHITE CHOCOLATE ICE CREAM:

1 recipe Walt's Dream (page 24)

7 ounces (200 g) white chocolate, chopped

1 cup (240 ml) raspberry jam

When the Marriage Equality Act passed in New York State (June 2011), we made a flavor called A Lovely Day using this white chocolate ice cream with broken-up pieces of rainbow cookies. The next year, we dyed the white chocolate ice cream purple and called it Ample Love! We make A Lovely Day—or Ample Love—every June for Pride Month.

SWITCH OUT the RASPBERRY JAM FOR your FAVORITE JAM. I make a great boysenberry blonde!

# SWEET CREAM AND COOKIES

1 (12-ounce/340-g) box or about 25 sandwich cookies, such as Back to Nature

1 recipe Walt's Dream (page 24)

Cookies and cream consistently ranks as one of the top five ice cream flavors across the country. There's something magical yet so simple about the combination of sweet cream and sandwich cookies. At Ample Hills, we've taste-tested nearly every Oreo-type knockoff out there (someone had to do it!), searching for the very best—the most chocolatey chocolate cookie and the creamiest cream filling—and our choice is Back to Nature Classic Creme Cookies. But please, experiment and find your favorite!

1.  Place 6 cookies in the freezer for 1 hour. Transfer the cookies to a small food processor and process them into crumbs. Or, for slightly more fun, place the cookies in a zip-top bag and pound them with your fist! Set this cookie "powder" aside.

2.  Prepare Walt's Dream according to the recipe directions. Transfer the cooled base to an ice cream maker and add the cookie powder. (This flavors the ice cream itself with the cookies and their cream filling.) Churn the ice cream according to the manufacturer's instructions.

3.  Break the remaining cookies into quarters. Transfer the ice cream to a storage container, folding in the cookie pieces as you do. Serve immediately or harden in your freezer for 8 to 12 hours for a more scoopable ice cream.

## KIDS' CORNER

Breaking up cookies for the ice cream is a fun way to involve your kids (or keep them busy while you're trying to cook)! Put a few cookies in a bag and have your child pulverize them in creative ways.

Brian's goal is to have customers complain that there are too many cookies in their scoops. Or as Christian says, Brian tries to choke people with cookies. Brian insists that the cookies be broken in quarters and meticulously layered throughout the ice cream. At home, you can add the cookies however you like: choking hazard or no.

Sweet Cream >>
and Cookies
(left)

<< Chocolate Milk
and Cookies
(page 42)

# CHOCOLATE MILK AND COOKIES

Chocolate milk meets sweet cream and cookies. Comfort food meets the ultimate comfort drink. This is a bestseller, especially for the under-twelve set.

1. Place 6 cookies in the freezer for 1 hour. Transfer the cookies to a small food processor and process them into crumbs. Or, for slightly more fun, place the cookies in a zip-top bag and pound them with your fist! Set this cookie "powder" aside.

2. Make the milk chocolate paste: In a small saucepan, bring ⅓ cup (80 ml) water to a boil over high heat. Remove the pan from the heat and add the sugar and cocoa powder, whisking vigorously to combine. Add the chocolate and whisk until melted. Set aside to cool.

3. Make the chocolate milk ice cream: Prepare Walt's Dream according to the recipe directions. Once the base reaches 165°F (75°C), remove it from the heat and mix in the cooled milk chocolate paste. Transfer the pan to the ice bath and let cool for 15 to 20 minutes. Pour the ice cream base through a wire-mesh strainer into a storage container and move to fridge for 1 to 2 hours, or until completely cool.

4. Transfer the cooled base to an ice cream maker and add the cookie powder. Churn the ice cream according to the manufacturer's instructions.

5. Break the remaining cookies into quarters. Transfer the ice cream to a storage container, folding in the cookie pieces as you do. Serve immediately or harden in your freezer for 8 to 12 hours for a more scoopable ice cream.

1 (12-ounce/340-g) box or about 25 sandwich cookies, such as Back to Nature

## FOR THE MILK CHOCOLATE PASTE:

¼ cup (50 g) organic cane sugar

⅓ cup (30 g) cocoa powder

2 ounces (55 g) semisweet chocolate, chopped

## FOR THE CHOCOLATE MILK ICE CREAM:

1 recipe Walt's Dream (page 24)

Whether in a sweet cream or chocolate base, there's something so scrumptious about cookies in ice cream. My two cents: Add them to peanut butter ice cream (see page 109), and WOWZA!

# SWEET AS HONEY

The simple beauty of Sweet as Honey was never supposed to be. You see, Brian started out to make a very different flavor, called Hundred Acre Wood. It was an homage to Winnie the Pooh made from a sweet cream base with pieces of honeycomb candy and organic gummy bears. Brian absolutely loved it, but most people complained that the gummy bears were too hard to chew in the ice cream. But Brian kept on—chewing, that is. The thing is, the gummy bears do work; you just have to leave them in your mouth for a little bit, to warm them up. Finally Brian relented and took out the gummy bears, and Sweet as Honey was born. And it continues to be one of our top ten sellers. (If you want to make Hundred Acre Wood, add 2 cups of gummy bears with the honeycomb candy.)

1. Make the honeycomb candy: Butter a 12-by-18-inch rimmed baking sheet and line it with parchment paper.

2. In a large saucepan, combine the sugar, honey, syrup, and ⅔ cup (160 ml) water. Whisk to combine. Clip a candy thermometer to the saucepan and set the pan over medium-high heat. Cook until the syrup reaches 305°F (150°C). (The syrup will bubble and spit, so please be careful.) Remove the pan from the heat and, wearing an oven mitt for protection, whisk in the baking soda. Whisk vigorously for a few moments to make sure you've incorporated all the little bits of baking soda, then stand back and watch the honeycomb grow.

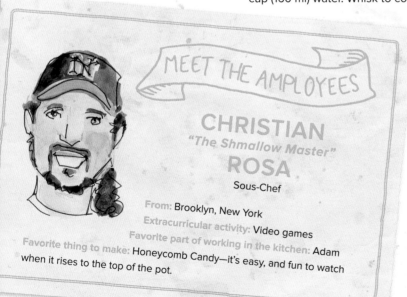

MEET THE AMPLOYEES

## CHRISTIAN
### *"The Shmallow Master"*
## ROSA
Sous-Chef

From: Brooklyn, New York
Extracurricular activity: Video games
Favorite part of working in the kitchen: Adam
Favorite thing to make: Honeycomb Candy—it's easy, and fun to watch when it rises to the top of the pot.

(continued)

Add Baking soda

## KIDS' CORNER

Remember building volcanoes for a science fair project? It's the same principle at work here. Adding the baking soda to the heated honey produces an abundance of carbon dioxide, causing the mixture to expand or erupt. In this case, however, the mixture is actually molten, so it needs to be observed at a safe distance.

Watch it grow!

We have honeycomb!

100% PURE
HONEY
QUEENS COUNTY
FARM MUSEUM
NET WT. 16 OZ.

3. When the honeycomb stops growing up the sides of the pot, gently pour it onto the prepared baking sheet. Let it cool. Refrigerate the candy for 30 minutes, then chop it into bite-size pieces.

4. Prepare Walt's Dream according to the recipe directions. Transfer the cooled base to an ice cream maker and churn it according to the manufacturer's instructions.

5. Transfer the ice cream to a storage container, folding in the pieces of honeycomb candy as you do. Use as much of the candy as you want; you won't necessarily need the whole batch. Serve immediately or harden in your freezer for 8 to 12 hours for a more scoopable ice cream.

# CARDAMOM BLISS

1 recipe Walt's Dream
(page 24)

½ teaspoon freshly ground
cardamom

7 ounces (200 g) white
chocolate, chopped

If you want to mimic Jackie's
favorite wedding truffles,
add sandwich cookies to this
flavor, in the same way that
they are added to Sweet Cream
and Cookies (page 40).

Jackie swoons for cardamom the way a cat swoons for catnip. When Jackie and Brian got married, Brian made white chocolate cardamom truffles enrobed in Oreo crumbs as take-away gifts. Ten years later, Jackie begged and pleaded for cardamom to be featured as one of Ample Hills' first twenty-four flavors. But Brian couldn't be persuaded. Not popular enough, he said. But wouldn't you think an ice cream–making husband would want to please his wife and make a cardamom flavor? Popularity be damned! A year later, in an effort to regain some marital harmony, Brian created Cardamom Bliss. Jackie tasted it and forgave him, and so far they have lived happily ever after.

1. Prepare Walt's Dream according to the recipe directions, adding the cardamom prior to heating the base. Once the base reaches 165°F (75°C), remove the pan from the heat and add the white chocolate. Stir until the white chocolate melts. Transfer the pan to the ice bath and let cool for 15 to 20 minutes. Pour the ice cream base through a wire-mesh strainer into a storage container and place in the refrigerator for 1 to 2 hours, or until completely cool.

2. Transfer the cooled base to an ice cream maker and churn it according to the manufacturer's instructions.

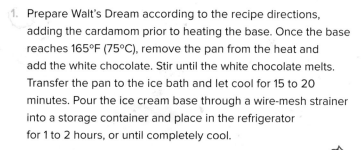

3. Transfer the ice cream to a storage container. Serve immediately or harden in your freezer for 8 to 12 hours for a more scoopable ice cream.

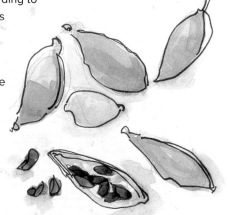

# COCONUT FUDGE

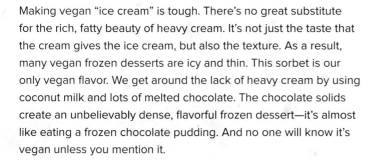

(VEGAN)

Making vegan "ice cream" is tough. There's no great substitute for the rich, fatty beauty of heavy cream. It's not just the taste that the cream gives the ice cream, but also the texture. As a result, many vegan frozen desserts are icy and thin. This sorbet is our only vegan flavor. We get around the lack of heavy cream by using coconut milk and lots of melted chocolate. The chocolate solids create an unbelievably dense, flavorful frozen dessert—it's almost like eating a frozen chocolate pudding. And no one will know it's vegan unless you mention it.

2½ cups (600 ml) unsweetened 100% coconut milk

⅔ cup (130 g) organic cane sugar

¼ cup (20 g) cocoa powder

¼ teaspoon salt

3 tablespoons golden syrup

8 ounces (225 g) semisweet chocolate, chopped

1. Prepare an ice bath in the sink or in a large heatproof bowl.

2. In a medium saucepan, combine the coconut milk, sugar, cocoa powder, salt, syrup, and ¾ cup (180 ml) water and whisk vigorously until smooth and combined. Clip a candy thermometer to the saucepan and set the pan over medium heat. Cook, stirring regularly with a rubber spatula and scraping the bottom of the pan to prevent the syrup from sticking and burning, until the mixture reaches 155°F (70°C).

3. Turn the heat to low and add the chocolate, stirring constantly until completely melted. Remove from the heat. Transfer the mixture to the ice bath and let cool for 15 to 20 minutes.

4. Transfer the cooled base to an ice cream maker and churn it according to the manufacturer's instructions.

5. Transfer the sorbet to a storage container. Serve immediately or harden in your freezer for 8 to 12 hours for a more scoopable sorbet.

> Feelin' spicy? Add 1 teaspoon ground red pepper flakes and 2 teaspoons ground cinnamon to this recipe for a kick that will knock your vegan socks off!

vegan

NOTE: Unlike Walt's Dream, which can be stored for up to 3 days in the refrigerator, you should churn this base as soon as it's been cooled in the ice bath. We've found that if we refrigerate the unchurned base overnight, all of the chocolate turns solid, like a pudding, and it makes it difficult to pour the base into the ice cream maker.

# STRAWBERRIES AND CREAM

1 pound (455 g) fresh or frozen strawberries

1¼ cups (250 g) organic cane sugar

1½ cups (360 ml) whole milk

¾ cup (90 g) skim milk powder

2 cups (480 ml) heavy cream

Ample Hills employees Christian and Adam named the walk-in fridge Christopher Walk-in and the walk-in freezer is Joaquin Freezer. When you visit our shop, please refer to them by their proper names.

Of course all strawberry ice cream is strawberries and cream, isn't it? (At least if it's made with heavy cream.) But somehow this name just makes it sound better, no? You'll note that we use more heavy cream than milk in this recipe—and also more skim milk powder than in our other recipes. That's because strawberries are composed predominantly of water, and we're trying to combat excess water by absorbing more of it into the skim milk powder and adding more milk solids with the heavy cream. It's important to macerate the strawberries by using sugar to draw as much water away from the fruit as possible. Also, we leave the egg yolks out of this recipe to make sure the flavor of the strawberries can really shine through. Because no egg yolks are used, we don't need to cook the mix.

1. Place the strawberries in a medium bowl and sprinkle ½ cup (100 g) of the sugar over them, tossing to coat them evenly. Cover the bowl with plastic wrap and set aside for 6 to 8 hours. Unwrap the bowl; you'll notice that the strawberries are now sitting in a pool of red, sugary water. Drain the strawberries in a colander in the sink.

2. Combine the milk, skim milk powder, remaining ¾ cup (150 g) sugar, and strawberries in a blender. Puree until smooth.

3. Pour the mixture into a bowl and add the cream. Stir to combine. Transfer the base to an ice cream maker and churn it according to the manufacturer's instructions.

4. Transfer the ice cream to a storage container. Serve immediately or harden in your freezer for 8 to 12 hours for a more scoopable ice cream.

2

# CURIOUSER

for when you dream
of taking the
road less traveled

WALT, WHITTY, AND PB race out of the park in search of the goblet!
They stop suddenly . . . and stare out over Grand Army Plaza, with the
Brooklyn Public Library to their right, the mighty Soldiers' and
Sailors' Arch straight ahead, and beyond, Neptune lounging in the
fountain pool. Walt doesn't move. Uh-oh. Witty doesn't move. He turns
to Witty and PB. "Um?" he mutters.

Nope, they haven't the foggiest idea of where to look for the goblet.

"The ice cream parlor?" asks PB.

"PB! Really?!" yells Whitty.

"We have to start somewhere," Walt concurs.

"And I can get seconds, thirds, and fourths!" PB exclaims.

At the old ice cream parlor, the grizzled owner leans down low and
beckons our merry adventurers with a tattooed finger. (Each finger is
tattooed with a different ice cream cone. This one's mint chocolate
chip.) "Come closer," he rasps. His breath smells of hot fudge and
walnuts. Maybe pecans. His voice crackles and chugs like a freight
train off the tracks.

"The woods. The deep, dark woods. Past the old
pignut hickory tree. Through the sweet-pepper
bushes. Talk to the ladybug. If she likes
you, she might help. I saw it once. I saw
the goblet. So beautiful."

Whitty grabs Walt. "This guy's nuts.
One too few scoops up there, you know?"

Back to the park and into the dark woods
go Walt, Whitty, and PB.

"Is that a pignut hickory?" Walt asks. "I think
it's a maple," Whitty replies. They're hopelessly
lost. But PB waves them over. He's sniffed it out.
"This way, guys!"

They pull back the leaves of the sweet-pepper bush,
and there, towering above them, are giant polka-dotted mushrooms. And
perched atop one of the mushrooms, eating a peanut butter and jelly
sandwich, is a ladybug.

"Hi, ladybug!" Walt waves, stumbles, and almost knocks the ladybug
off the mushroom.

"We're looking for an ice cream goblet that never runs out," says Witty.

"I'm busy," says the ladybug, as she takes another bite of her sandwich. "Go away."

Witty clucks, "But we need your help! This old man said you could help. Can you?!"

The ladybug scuttles away from them. PB sniffles. He can tell the ladybug doesn't like them. And won't help them.

Walt puts a hand on PB and pleads with the ladybug. "Please. We've come a long way. PB here won't forgive us if we don't at least try to find the goblet."

"PB, like peanut butter? Peanut Butter the Pig!" the ladybug exclaims. "That's my favorite sandwich. Not the pig part, but the peanut butter. I'm a vegetarian." She holds up her sandwich. "See? I love peanut butter and jelly sandwiches." The ladybug flaps her wings and hovers in front of PB's snout. "You're so cute, I could just eat you up!"

PB blushes. "The goblet isn't here," the ladybug explains. "At least not now. It might have been here a long time ago, though."

The ladybug tears off a large chunk of the polka-dotted mushroom and hands it to PB. And since the mushroom looks like food, PB does the only reasonable thing he can think of. He puts it in his mouth. "Wait! Small bites, PB!" she exclaims. PB spits the mushroom out.

The ladybug continues, "The top half makes you go forward. The bottom half makes you go back."

"Back where?!" Whitty wants to know.

"In time, of course." She blows PB a kiss. "Follow the peanuts, PB."

"But how far back should we go?" PB asks. But the ladybug has vanished.

"Where did she go?" Walt asks.

"I don't like mushrooms," Whitty says.

"Just pretend it's ice cream," PB says as he hands Walt and Whitty pieces of the mushroom. "A little bite first? All together, on three. One, two, three—Here we go!"

# BANANAMON

## FOR THE BANANA ICE CREAM:

1½ cups (360 ml) whole milk

¾ cup (90 g) skim milk powder

¾ cup (150 g) organic cane sugar

1½ teaspoons vanilla extract

1¼ teaspoons ground cinnamon

1 pound (455 g) ripe peeled fresh bananas

2 cups (480 ml) heavy cream

1 (12-ounce/340-g) box or about 25 vanilla wafer cookies

Long before Ample Hills was even an idea, this was Jackie's other favorite flavor (besides Cardamom Bliss, page 48). Summers at Trout Lake always included making this twisted ode to banana pudding. It's a creamy banana-and-cinnamon ice cream, with loads of crushed vanilla wafer cookies in every bite. As with Strawberries and Cream (page 50), we leave the egg yolks out of this recipe to allow the fruit flavor to shine through, and no eggs means you don't have to cook the base.

1. Make the banana ice cream: In a blender, combine the milk, skim milk powder, sugar, vanilla, cinnamon, and bananas and blend until smooth. Transfer the mixture to a bowl and add the cream. Stir until combined.

2. Transfer the base to an ice cream maker and churn it according to the manufacturer's instructions.

3. Break the vanilla wafer cookies into quarters. Transfer the ice cream to a storage container, gently folding in the cookie pieces as you do. Serve immediately or harden in your freezer for 8 to 12 hours for a more scoopable ice cream.

# TROUT LAKE AND BANANAMON

Jackie and her family have been vacationing in the Adirondacks for almost forty years, at a cabin community called Trout Lake Club. Jackie brought Brian to Trout Lake for the first time in the late 1990s. There are really only two reasons someone would get an invite to Trout Lake Club:

1. They are marriage material, or
2. They have a special talent or skill the people at Trout Lake will truly appreciate.

At that point, Jackie wasn't sure yet about the marriage part. What she was sure of, however, was that Brian could produce some amazing ice cream, cakes, and brownies. And that first summer, he did not disappoint. Every other night a communal feast with a specific theme would occur at a different family's cabin, and Jackie's family would enter a cabin with her mother's four-and-a-half-hour Indian chicken dish and Brian's Bananamon ice cream. Jackie's mother couldn't be any happier or prouder to have her future son-in-law following in her culinary footsteps. (Jackie's mom's cookies can be found on page 91 in the recipe for Nonna D's Oatmeal Lace.)

Brian's ice cream quickly became a highly anticipated staple. Jackie and Brian would brainstorm creative flavor ideas while relaxing on the lake. The afternoon would be spent churning the hand-crank ice cream maker on the porch of their cabin, recruiting anyone who happened to paddle or row past. Brian's ice cream was a big hit, and so was he. Brian was invited back year after year, and he eventually became marriage material.

# NANATELLA

1 recipe banana ice cream (page 56)

**FOR THE NUTELLA SWIRL:**

1 (13-ounce/370-g) jar Nutella

½ cup (120 ml) heavy cream

Our general manager, Eric, often asks the kitchen staff to save him extra ice cream base so he can experiment with making flavors at home. Then he'll come in and share his latest concoction: a carrot-cake-and-cream-cheese ice cream, or a Pop-Tarts-and-rainbow-sprinkles ice cream . . . We may yet make the carrot cake flavor, but we'll probably pass on the Pop Tarts. Nanatella is far and away his best creation: a smooth banana ice cream with heaping swirls of Nutella. It's a shop favorite. Bananas, chocolate, and hazelnut—who knew? Well, Eric did.

1.  Prepare the banana ice cream according to the recipe directions. Transfer the cooled base to an ice cream maker and churn it according to the manufacturer's instructions.

2.  While the ice cream is churning, make the Nutella swirl: In a medium bowl, whisk together the Nutella and cream. The cream should thin out the Nutella so it can be spooned into the ice cream. It should pour off the spoon like honey.

3.  Transfer the banana base to a storage container, gently folding in heaping spoonfuls of the Nutella swirl as you do, softly lifting and spinning it throughout the ice cream. Be careful not to overmix. Serve immediately or harden in your freezer for 8 to 12 hours for a more scoopable ice cream.

## MEET THE AMPLOYEES

### ERIC
*"Can You Be My Hand Model?"*
### WU

General Manager and Facebook Photographer

From: San Francisco, California
Favorite thing to make: Ice cream on the ice cream bike. It's magical!
Best comment from a customer: Little boy sitting at the counter happily licking his cone, saying, "I want to live here!"

<< Bananamon
(page 56)

Nanatella >>
(left)

# GATHER 'ROUND THE CAMPFIRE

Christian gets his nick-name, "The Shmallow Master," from this flavor. Cooking marshmallows on parchment paper in a convection oven is a tricky business, but Christian perfected the art, and this flavor became a bestseller.

Lots of people make s'mores ice cream, but they often miss a key flavor. If you make a chocolate ice cream with ribbons of marshmallow and graham cracker crumbs, it might taste good, but it won't taste like a s'more. What's missing? The fire! The charred caramelized sugar of the toasted marshmallows—that's the secret to a great s'more. When we make this flavor at the shop, we toast hundreds and hundreds of marshmallows, then puree them to make a toasted-marshmallow ice cream. The smoke and smell of the burning marshmallows fills the shop for hours. We often have customers offer to call the fire department. You may have to open a nearby window, but trust us: This flavor is worth a little smoke inhalation.

1. Make the toasted marshmallow ice cream: Preheat the oven to 400°F (205°C). Butter a baking sheet and line it with parchment paper. Prepare an ice bath in your sink or in a large heatproof bowl.

2. In a medium saucepan, combine the sugar, skim milk powder, and milk. Stir with a hand mixer or whisk until smooth. Make sure the skim milk powder is wholly dissolved into the mixture and that no lumps remain (any remaining sugar granules will dissolve over the heat). Stir in the cream.

3. Clip a candy thermometer to the saucepan and set the pan over medium heat. Cook, stirring often with a rubber spatula and scraping the bottom of the pan to prevent sticking and burning, until the mixture reaches 110°F (45°C), 5 to 10 minutes. Remove the pan from the heat.

4. Place the egg yolks in a medium bowl. While whisking, slowly pour ½ cup (120 ml) of the hot milk mixture into the egg yolks to temper them. Continue to whisk slowly until the mixture is an even color and consistency, then whisk the egg-yolk mixture back into the remaining milk mixture.

5. Return the pan to the stovetop over medium heat and continue cooking the mixture, stirring often, until it reaches 165°F (75°C), 5 to 10 minutes more.

6. Transfer the pan to the prepared ice bath and let cool for 15 to 20 minutes, stirring occasionally. Pour the ice cream base through a wire-mesh strainer into a storage container and place in the refrigerator for 1 to 2 hours, or until completely cool.

7. While the base is cooling, toast the marshmallows: Line up the marshmallows on the prepared baking sheet, leaving a couple of inches of space between the marshmallows and the sides of the pan (they have a way of expanding and melting over the sides). Bake until browned, about 15 minutes. If you want them almost black, then go for it. It's up to you.

8. Remove the pan of ice cream base from the refrigerator, and use a rubber spatula to gently slide the burnt marshmallows into the base. Be careful not to let the molten marshmallow drip on your hands. It's very sticky and hard to work with, so move quickly before it sets and becomes too hard. Use a handheld immersion blender to break up and distribute the toasted marshmallow in the base. If you don't have an immersion blender, transfer the base and marshmallows to a food processor and pulse until combined and smooth.

9. Transfer the ice cream base to a storage container and refrigerate until ready to use.

10. Make the graham cracker crust: Butter a 12-by-18-inch rimmed baking sheet and line it with parchment paper.

11. In a large bowl, combine the graham cracker crumbs, sugar, skim milk powder, and cinnamon. Whisk to combine.

(continued)

### FOR THE GRAHAM CRACKER CRUST:

Butter for the baking sheet

3 cups (420 g) ground graham cracker crumbs

½ cup (100 g) organic cane sugar

¼ cup (30 g) skim milk powder

½ teaspoon ground cinnamon

¾ cup (180 g) unsalted butter, melted

2 ounces (55 g) cream cheese

1 teaspoon vanilla extract

### FOR THE CREAMY MILK CHOCOLATE SWIRL:

6 ounces (170 g) milk chocolate, chopped

½ cup (120 ml) heavy cream

Feelin' fiery? Make s'mores with crack cookies! (see page 147)

12. In a small saucepan, heat the butter and cream cheese over low heat until just melted, stirring to combine. Add the vanilla. Pour the cream cheese mixture over the dry ingredients and work them together with your hands.

13. Spread the graham cracker mixture over the prepared baking sheet, and press it into a compact, even layer about ½ inch (12 mm) thick. (The goal here is to really pack the crust together so the butter and cream cheese bond all of the dry ingredients together. This way you can chop it up later, and the crust won't break apart into a thousand little crumbs.) Place the baking sheet in the freezer for 1 hour.

14. Chop the graham cracker crust into bite-size pieces and set aside.

15. Make the creamy milk chocolate swirl: Place the milk chocolate in a heatproof bowl. In a small saucepan, heat the heavy cream over medium-high heat until it just starts to bubble, then pour it over the milk chocolate. Stir gently until fully melted and combined.

16. Transfer the cooled base to an ice cream maker and churn it according to the manufacturer's instructions.

17. When the ice cream is nearly finished churning, open the lid and add the crust pieces. Use as much of the crust as you want; you won't necessarily need the whole batch. Finish churning, then transfer the ice cream to a storage container, gently folding in heaping spoonfuls of the milk chocolate swirl as you do, softly lifting and spinning it throughout the ice cream. Be careful not to overmix, or you might end up with chocolate marshmallow ice cream rather than marshmallow ice cream with a chocolate swirl. Serve immediately or harden in your freezer for 8 to 12 hours for a more scoopable ice cream.

# NO MORE MONKEYS JUMPING ON THE BREAD!

This is a hard flavor for us to make at the shop. Whenever we bake fresh, hot monkey bread, it's just too damn difficult not to eat it all before it cools and we chop it up into the ice cream. And honestly, monkey bread never tastes quite as good as it does the moment it comes out of the oven. This flavor of ice cream tries (but mostly fails) to capture the joy of pulling gooey, hot, brown-sugar-dripping cinnamon biscuit balls off a mountain of fresh monkey bread. To have the best of both worlds, make this ice cream, but save some of the monkey bread. When you're ready to serve it, nuke a big chunk of the monkey bread. Serve the ice cream on top, and you might just have the best sundae in the universe.

1.  Make the cream cheese ice cream: Prepare Walt's Dream according to the recipe directions. When the mixture reaches 165°F (75°C), remove the pan from the heat and mix in the cream cheese and vanilla. Using a whisk or hand mixer, stir vigorously to make sure the cream cheese melts and combines smoothly.

2.  Transfer the pan to the ice bath and let cool for 15 to 20 minutes, stirring occasionally. Pour the ice cream base through a wire-mesh strainer into a storage container and place in the refrigerator for 1 to 2 hours, or until completely cool.

3.  Make the monkey bread: Preheat the oven to 350°F (175°C). Butter a 12-by-18-inch baking sheet and line it with parchment paper.

(continued)

## FOR THE CREAM CHEESE ICE CREAM:

**1 recipe Walt's Dream (page 24)**

**4 ounces (115 g) cream cheese**

**2 teaspoons vanilla extract**

## FOR THE MONKEY BREAD:

**Butter for the baking sheet**

**1 tablespoon ground cinnamon**

**¾ cup (150 g) organic cane sugar**

**2 (16-ounce/455-g) cans buttermilk biscuit dough (see Note)**

**1 cup (240 g) unsalted butter**

**1¾ cups (385 g) packed dark brown sugar**

**1 teaspoon vanilla extract**

Note: We recommend Immaculate Baking Company's Buttermilk Biscuits.

4. In a medium bowl, combine the cinnamon and cane sugar. Chop the biscuit dough into 1-inch pieces and roll each piece in the cinnamon-sugar mixture. Place the coated dough balls on the prepared baking sheet, piling the pieces together and smushing them into one another. They can end up two or three pieces deep, but just make sure you've laid out the pieces fairly evenly. Aim for a smooth plateau, not a mountain range—otherwise, the bread won't cook evenly.

5. In a small saucepan, melt the butter with the brown sugar and vanilla, stirring to combine. Pour the mixture evenly over the monkey bread. Bake for 30 minutes.

6. Remove the monkey bread and set it aside to cool. If you haven't eaten it all at this point, wrap it in foil and refrigerate it for 1 hour. Then chop the monkey bread into bite-size pieces and set aside.

7. Transfer the cooled base to an ice cream maker and churn it according to the manufacturer's instructions.

8. Transfer the ice cream to a storage container, folding in the pieces of monkey bread as you do. Use as much of the monkey bread as you want; you won't necessarily need the whole batch. Serve immediately or harden in your freezer for 8 to 12 hours for a more scoopable ice cream.

## KIDS' CORNER

Instead of chopping the biscuit dough into uniform pieces, have your kids help rip the dough into small pieces and coat them with the cinnamon-sugar mixture. Count the pieces as you go. It's fun and not *too* messy.

MEET THE AMPLOYEES

### ADAM
*"Full Sweet Cream and Dishes"*
### LIPPERT
Sous-Chef II

From: Des Moines, Iowa
Extracurricular activity: Bike riding
Favorite part of working in the kitchen: Christian
Favorite thing to make: Graham cracker crust
Favorite thing to eat: Monkey bread

# BREAKFAST TRASH

At Ample Hills, we pride ourselves on making things from scratch, using as many organic ingredients as possible and creating an all-natural ice cream that doesn't include items you can't pronounce. Well, throw all of that out the window with this flavor. Breakfast Trash is brazenly unnatural. It's a celebration of that guiltiest of guilty pleasures: sugar cereal. We steep Cap'n Crunch, Corn Pops, and Frosted Flakes in whole milk, pulling all the corny goodness, sugar, and 127 artificial flavors out of them. We strain out the soggy mess and then mix in Froot Loops and Fruity Pebbles, creating the most amazing breakfast-cereal-flavored ice cream you can imagine! For dessert. Where it belongs.

1. Make the cereal ice cream: Prepare an ice bath in the sink or in a large heatproof bowl.

2. In a large saucepan, heat the milk over medium-high heat until it starts to steam, 10 to 15 minutes. Remove the pan from the heat and stir in the cereals. Cover the pan and let the cereal steep for 20 minutes. Pour the mixture through a wire-mesh strainer into a bowl, pressing down on the cereal in the strainer to extract as much milk as possible. Don't worry if some of the cereal "pulp" pushes through into the ice cream. That's totally OK. Return the cereal-infused milk to the saucepan.

3. Add the sugar and skim milk powder. Stir with a hand mixer or whisk until smooth. Make sure the skim milk powder is wholly dissolved into the mixture and that no lumps remain (any remaining sugar granules will dissolve over the heat). Stir in the cream.

(continued)

## FOR THE CEREAL ICE CREAM:

3 cups (720 ml) whole milk

1 cup (40 g) Cap'n Crunch

½ cup (20 g) Corn Pops

½ cup (20 g) Frosted Flakes

½ cup (100 g) organic cane sugar

½ cup (60 g) skim milk powder

1⅔ cups (400 ml) heavy cream

2 egg yolks

## FOR THE FRUITY BREAKFAST MIX-IN:

Butter for the baking sheet

1½ cups (60 g) Froot Loops

1½ cups (60 g) Fruity Pebbles

⅓ cup (40 g) skim milk powder

1 tablespoon organic cane sugar

½ cup (120 g) unsalted butter, melted

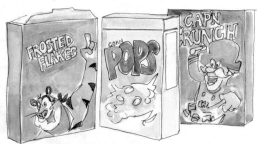

4. Clip a candy thermometer to the saucepan and set the pan over medium heat. Cook, stirring often with a rubber spatula and scraping the bottom of the pan to prevent sticking and burning, until the mixture reaches 110°F (45°C), 5 to 10 minutes. Remove the pan from the heat.

5. Place the egg yolks in a medium bowl. While whisking, slowly pour ½ cup (120 ml) of the hot milk mixture into the egg yolks to temper them. Continue to whisk slowly until the mixture is an even color and consistency, then whisk the egg-yolk mixture back into the remaining milk mixture.

6. Return the pan to the stovetop over medium heat and continue cooking the mixture, stirring often, until it reaches 165°F (75°C), 5 to 10 minutes more.

7. Transfer the pan to the prepared ice bath and let cool for 15 to 20 minutes, stirring occasionally. Pour the ice cream base through a wire-mesh strainer into a storage container and place in the refrigerator for 1 to 2 hours, or until completely cool.

8. Make the fruity breakfast mix-in: Preheat the oven to 275°F (135°C). Butter a 12-by-18-inch baking sheet and line it with parchment paper.

9. In a large bowl, crush the Froot Loops and Fruity Pebbles with your hands to about half their original size. The goal here isn't to pulverize them into dust (though a little cereal dust is OK, as it will help bind everything together later on). Add the skim milk powder and sugar and toss to combine. Pour the butter over the cereal mix and work it together with your hands, squeezing it into clumps and then breaking it apart, almost like kneading dough.

10. Spread the mixture evenly over the prepared baking sheet and bake for 15 to 20 minutes, until the cereal just begins to toast and turn brown. Set aside to cool completely.

11. Transfer the cooled base to an ice cream maker and churn it according to the manufacturer's instructions.

12. Transfer the ice cream to a storage container, folding in pieces of the fruity breakfast mix-in as you do. Use as much of the mix-in as you want; you won't necessarily need the whole batch. Serve immediately or harden in your freezer for 8 to 12 hours for a more scoopable ice cream.

Breakfast Trash can be altered using a limitless combination of cereals. Brian made a cocoa edition using Cocoa Krispies and Cookie Crisp. That was the first time Brian ever said, "This is the best thing I ever made," and insisted that Lauren make him a birthday cake using it. Brian has subsequently said this about every new flavor.

# THE MUNCHIES

If Brian had to pick one favorite flavor, it might just be The Munchies. It's the perfect combination of salty and sweet. We steep salted pretzels in our sweet cream base, so the ice cream takes on the malty, salty beauty of great pretzels. Then we add a combination of potato chips, Ritz crackers, and even more pretzels. Oh, and we throw in some M&M's for a little chocolatey finish.

1. Make the pretzel ice cream: Prepare an ice bath in the sink or in a large heatproof bowl.

2. In a large saucepan, heat the milk over medium-high heat until it starts to steam, about 10 to 15 minutes. Remove the pan from the heat and stir in the pretzels. Cover the pan and let the pretzels steep for 20 minutes. Pour the mixture through a wire-mesh strainer into a bowl, pressing down on the pretzels to extract as much milk as possible. Don't worry if some of the pretzel "pulp" pushes through into the ice cream. That's totally OK. Return the pretzel-infused milk to the saucepan.

3. Add the sugar and skim milk powder. Stir with a hand mixer or whisk until smooth. Make sure the skim milk powder is wholly dissolved into the mixture and that no lumps remain (any remaining sugar granules will dissolve over the heat). Stir in the cream.

4. Clip a candy thermometer to the saucepan and set the pan over medium heat. Cook, stirring often with a rubber spatula and scraping the bottom of the pan to prevent sticking and burning, until the mixture reaches 110°F (45°C), 5 to 10 minutes. Remove the pan from the heat.

5. Place the egg yolks in a medium bowl. While whisking, slowly pour ½ cup (120 ml) of the hot milk mixture into the egg yolks to temper them. Continue to whisk slowly until the mixture is an even color and consistency, then whisk the egg-yolk mixture back into the remaining milk mixture.

## FOR THE PRETZEL ICE CREAM:

3 cups (720 ml) whole milk

1½ cups (90 g) mini salted pretzels

¾ cup (150 g) organic cane sugar

½ cup (60 g) skim milk powder

1⅔ cups (400 ml) heavy cream

2 egg yolks

## FOR THE MUNCHIES MIX-IN:

1 generous cup (40 g) Ritz crackers

1 generous cup (60 g) salted mini pretzels

1 generous cup (30 g) salted potato chips

½ cup (60 g) skim milk powder

1 cup (200 g) organic cane sugar

½ cup (120 g) unsalted butter, melted

8 ounces (225 g) M&M's, chopped

(continued)

6. Return the pan to the stovetop over medium heat and continue cooking the mixture, stirring often, until it reaches 165°F (75°C), 5 to 10 minutes more.

7. Transfer the pan to the prepared ice bath and let cool for 15 to 20 minutes, stirring occasionally. Pour the ice cream base through a wire-mesh strainer into a storage container and place in the refrigerator for 1 to 2 hours, or until completely cool.

8. Make the munchies mix-in: Preheat the oven to 275°F (135°C). Butter a 12-by-18-inch baking sheet and line it with parchment paper.

9. In a large bowl, using your hands, break up the crackers, pretzels, and potato chips into pieces about a quarter of their original size. The goal here isn't to pulverize them into dust (though a little dust is OK, as it will help bind everything together later on). Add the skim milk powder and sugar and toss to combine. Pour the butter over the mixture and work it together with your hands, squeezing it into clumps and breaking it apart, almost like kneading dough.

10. Spread the mixture evenly over the prepared baking sheet and bake for 20 minutes, until the mixture just begins to toast and turn brown. Set aside to cool completely.

11. Transfer the cooled base to an ice cream maker and churn it according to the manufacturer's instructions.

12. Transfer the ice cream to a storage container, folding in the munchies mix-in and M&M's as you do. Use as much of the mix-in as you want; you won't necessarily need the whole batch. Serve immediately or harden in your freezer for 8 to 12 hours for a more scoopable ice cream.

When you're feeling a bit more sophisticated, the pretzel ice cream is simply divine on its own!

# I WANT TO MARRY THIS!

At Ample Hills, we're always experimenting with bacon, trying to create the ultimate bacon ice cream. When we made this version and let the staff taste it, our assistant manager, Katie, exclaimed, "I want to marry this!" The name stuck. It's a maple ice cream with pieces of bacon bark coated in semisweet chocolate. When the flavor premiered in the shop, our artist in residence, Lauren, drew a sign depicting Katie walking down the aisle with a slice of bacon. Marital bliss. When Katie saw the flavor and sign make their debut, tears welled up in her eyes.

1. Make the maple ice cream: Prepare an ice bath in the sink or in a large heatproof bowl.

2. In a medium saucepan, combine the sugar, skim milk powder, and milk. Stir with a hand mixer or whisk until smooth. Make sure the skim milk powder is wholly dissolved into the mixture and that no lumps remain (any remaining sugar granules will dissolve over the heat). Stir in the maple syrup and cream.

3. Clip a candy thermometer to the saucepan and set the pan over medium heat. Cook, stirring often with a rubber spatula and scraping the bottom of the pan to prevent sticking and burning, until the mixture reaches 110°F (45°C), 5 to 10 minutes. Remove the pan from the heat.

4. Place the egg yolks in a medium bowl. While whisking, slowly pour ½ cup (120 ml) of the hot milk mixture into the egg yolks to temper them. Continue to whisk slowly until the mixture is an even color and consistency, then whisk the egg-yolk mixture back into the remaining milk mixture.

(continued)

## FOR THE MAPLE ICE CREAM:

2 tablespoons organic cane sugar

½ cup plus 2 tablespoons (75 g) skim milk powder

1⅓ cups (315 ml) whole milk

¾ cup (180 ml) grade B maple syrup

2 cups (480 ml) heavy cream

2 egg yolks

## FOR THE BACON BARK:

Butter for the baking sheet

1 pound (455 g) bacon

14 tablespoons (210 g) unsalted butter

2¼ cups (450 g) organic cane sugar

½ cup (110 g) packed dark brown sugar

2 teaspoons salt

2½ teaspoons vanilla extract

½ teaspoon baking soda

8 ounces (225 g) semisweet chocolate, chopped

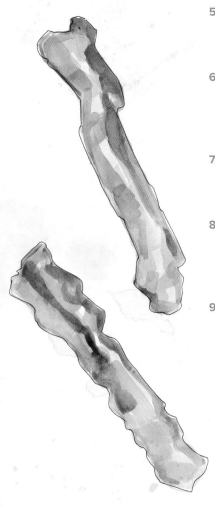

5. Return the pan to the stovetop over medium heat and continue cooking the mixture, stirring often, until it reaches 165°F (75°C), 5 to 10 minutes more.

6. Transfer the pan to the prepared ice bath and let cool for 15 to 20 minutes, stirring occasionally. Pour the ice cream base through a wire-mesh strainer into a storage container and place in the refrigerator for 1 to 2 hours, or until completely cool.

7. Make the bacon bark: Preheat the oven to 400°F (205°C). Butter two 12-by-18-inch rimmed baking sheets and line them with parchment paper.

8. On one baking sheet, lay out the bacon strips in a single layer. Bake until crispy, about 15 minutes. Reserve ¼ cup (60 ml) of the bacon grease from the pan and discard the rest or reserve it for another use. Let cool, then break the bacon into small pieces and set aside.

9. In a medium saucepan, combine the butter, cane sugar, brown sugar, salt, reserved bacon grease, and ¼ cup (60 ml) water. Clip a candy thermometer to the pan and set the pan over medium-high heat. Cook, stirring, until just combined, then continue to cook without stirring until the mixture reaches 305°F (150°C). Be very careful—the toffee will bubble up as it boils. It is very hot and will cause serious burns if it spatters on you. Using oven mitts, remove the pan from the heat, remove the thermometer, and add the vanilla. The vanilla might spatter when it hits the hot toffee, so be careful. Add the baking soda and whisk vigorously for a few seconds to combine. Then add the bacon pieces and fold into the toffee. Pour the toffee evenly onto the prepared baking sheet.

10. Before the toffee cools, sprinkle the chocolate across the top. Wait a minute or two, then use a spatula to spread the now melted chocolate across the top of the toffee. Let cool completely, then refrigerate for 1 hour, until the toffee has hardened. Chop the toffee into bite-size pieces and set aside.

11. Transfer the cooled base to an ice cream maker and churn it according to the manufacturer's instructions.

12. Transfer the ice cream to a storage container, folding in the pieces of bacon bark as you do. Use as much of the bacon bark as you want; you won't necessarily need the whole batch. Serve immediately or harden in your freezer for 8 to 12 hours for a more scoopable ice cream.

MEET THE AMPLOYEES

## KATIE
*"Scoopin' Is a Lifestyle"*
## THOMPSON
Manager

**From:** Chicago, Illinois
**Extracurricular activity:** Professional ice cream eater
**Flavor combination suggestion:** Nonna D's Oatmeal Lace and Ooey Gooey Butter Cake
**Fun fact:** Katie has an ice cream cone tattoo, drawn by Lauren, on her wrist. She's pretty committed.

Say YES to bacon bark!

3

# NOSTALGIC

for when you
want to take a trip
down memory lane

WALT AND WHITTY AND PB tumble through time. Walt stretches out his legs and glides down, pretending he's a paper airplane. Whitty screams and clucks and flaps his wings, terrified. PB somersaults. They fall past kids with big hair playing Pac-Man in the eighties. They fall past families eating fondue, listening to Peter, Paul, and Mary sing "Puff, the Magic Dragon" in the seventies. They fall past tie-dyed teens playing Twister and watching *Star Trek* on TV in the sixties. They fall past a five-year-old girl in a poodle skirt riding in the back of her daddy's T-Bird convertible, singing along to Buddy Holly in the fifties.

THUD! They land on the floor.

Dazed, it takes them a few minutes to sit up and realize where they are. It's the ice cream parlor. *Their* ice cream parlor. But it looks different. Better. Newer. Cleaner. And it smells different.

A dozen freshly jerked ice cream sodas and egg creams line the counter. Bobby-soxers swivel about on their wooden stools, kicking their feet out, sharing secrets, sneezing and giggling as they breathe in the fizzy bubbles bouncing from their drinks. Thousands of bubbles escape, take flight, and blow about the soda shop. The scents of cherry phosphates, chocolate egg creams, and orange crushes mingle in the cool air. The room is alive with the aromas of fruit, chocolate, and all things sweet and wonderful.

Walt, Whitty, and PB smile as they breathe in the ice cream shop. They sit at the counter.

On the walls are beautiful illustrated signs advertising chocolate malteds, black cow floats, and something called a Knickerbocker Glory Sundae. "I want that one," PB says. "But I think I'll have a black cow float first."

"Everything is so beautiful! So much more beautiful than before—or than later, I guess," says Walt. "It's magic. Like being in a painting. A scratch-and-sniff painting."

A young soda jerk in a crisp white uniform turns to them and hands them a menu. On his finger is a tattoo of a chocolate chip cone. He smiles at the cow, chicken, and pig sitting in front of him. He's sixty-five years younger. And he has dimples that light up his face. "Thanks," PB says. "I like the chocolate chip cone tattoo. But

I don't think you should get them on all your fingers.
It'll look kind of messy. Don't you agree, Whitty?"

The soda jerk laughs. That and the smile are two
things Walt, Whitty, and PB never saw him do as an
old man. "You fellas look a little lost. What can I
help you with?"

"What year is it?" Walt asks.

"I'd like a black cow float, please," PB says.

"Do you know where the purple goblet is?" Whitty wants
to know.

"The year is 1947," the soda jerk says. "Never saw a purple
goblet, but we do have some beautiful glass sundae bowls that are
tinted kind of bluish-green. Want to take a look?"

"It's a magic goblet. It never gets empty. The ice cream keeps
filling it up forever," Walt explains.

"Magic, you say?" The soda jerk ponders this for a moment. Then he
leans down close to them and whispers, "Well, if you ever find it,
and it works, will you do me a favor? Will you keep it a secret?
Something like that would be bad for business, right?"

The soda jerk turns to PB. "Let me whip up that black cow float for
you." He grabs a tall glass and prepares a towering black cow float
in front of Walt, Whitty, and PB. There are layers of chocolate
syrup, root beer, ice cream, and whipped cream. Walt and PB
take big sips. So delicious.

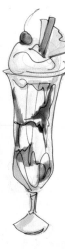

"The ladybug said to follow the peanuts," PB says to the
soda jerk.

"A talking ladybug, too? Hmmph. Well, we have some peanuts
for topping sundaes, if you want."

"Do you know what she meant by 'follow the peanuts'?" PB asks.

"I'll tell you one thing. All the peanuts in the city come
from underneath the bridge. In the anchorage. That's where
they keep them. Something about the cool air, they say—keeps
them fresh," the soda jerk replies.

"That's it!" PB shouts. He slurps down his black cow float. "Can
I get a Knickerbocker Glory Sundae to go please? With peanuts!"

# BUBBLEGUM

1 recipe Walt's Dream
(page 24)

½ teaspoon vanilla extract

½ teaspoon orange extract

½ teaspoon lemon extract

¼ teaspoon raspberry
extract

¼ teaspoon cinnamon syrup

Red food coloring (see Note)

Store-bought gumballs
(optional)

## KIDS' CORNER

Have your child measure out
these extracts separately in
small bowls before adding
them to the mix. Measure
each amount and smell—
can they distinguish the
different flavors? Then mix
them together and—poof!—
the fragrance is transformed.
Smell the extracts now!

When Brian was a kid, his favorite flavor of ice cream was
Swenson's Bubblegum. It was pink and had great big penny
gumballs in it. He would eat the ice cream first and save the
gumballs for the end, going home with a wad of eight or nine
gumballs, chomping away on them in the backseat. One of
Brian's goals with Ample Hills was to re-create that flavor, but with
all-natural ingredients. It proved a lot harder than he expected.
What is the flavor of bubblegum itself? Of course these days,
it's an artificial flavor. But it had to originate somewhere—it
had to be based on something real. After some research and
experimentation, Brian figured it out! But alas, if you add all-natural
pieces of gum to your ice cream, they will disintegrate when you
chew them. We're not sure why, but perhaps there's something
in an artificial gumball that holds it all together, even after being
frozen in ice cream.

1. Prepare Walt's Dream according to the recipe directions. After
   cooling the base in the ice bath, add the extracts and syrup and
   stir to combine. Add the food coloring drop by drop to achieve
   the desired color.

2. Transfer the cooled base to an ice cream maker and churn
   it according to the manufacturer's instructions.

3. Transfer the ice cream to a storage container,
   folding in the gumballs (if using) as you do.
   Serve immediately or harden in your freezer
   for 8 to 12 hours for a more scoopable
   ice cream.

NOTE: There are many online sources for all-
natural food coloring. We use Nature's Flavors.
India Tree is another great source. Be careful
when adding all-natural food dyes, as they do
tend to impart some flavor. Experiment by
adding them bit by bit, mixing in just
enough to get the color you want.

# ORANGE DREAMSICLE
(DAIRY-FREE)

This sorbet tastes like summertime in Florida. It's a comforting favorite that will transport you back in time. It's light, refreshing, and yet, with an added splash of Cointreau, just a little bit grown-up, too. Perfect for sunny summer afternoons, or better yet, for bleak, depressing, snowed-in days when you find yourself in need of a reminder that summer will come again . . . eventually.

¼ cup (60 ml) golden syrup

½ cup (100 g) organic cane sugar

4 egg whites

2½ cups (600 ml) orange juice

1 vanilla bean

2 tablespoons Cointreau

¼ teaspoon orange extract

½ teaspoon vanilla extract

1. Prepare an ice bath in the sink or in a large heatproof bowl.

2. In a medium saucepan, combine the syrup, sugar, egg whites, orange juice, and 1 cup (240 ml) water. Whisk vigorously to break apart the egg whites and combine. Halve the vanilla bean lengthwise and gently scrape out the seeds. Add the seeds and pod to the saucepan.

3. Clip a candy thermometer to the saucepan and set the pan over medium heat. Cook, stirring regularly with a rubber spatula and scraping the bottom of the pan to prevent sticking and burning, until the mixture reaches 165°F (75°C), 5 to 10 minutes more. Transfer the pan to the prepared ice bath and let cool for 15 to 20 minutes.

4. Pour the base through a wire-mesh strainer into a bowl. Add the Cointreau and the extracts and stir to combine.

5. Transfer the base to an ice cream maker and churn it according to the manufacturer's instructions.

6. Transfer the sorbet to a storage container. Serve immediately or harden in your freezer for 8 to 12 hours for a more scoopable sorbet.

# COTTON CANDY

1 recipe Walt's Dream
(page 24)

2 teaspoons Nature's Flavors
cotton candy flavor extract

Blue food coloring

This is the most popular kids' flavor in our shop. When we took it away for a few weeks one time, the children in the area revolted. They picketed the shop, started a letter-writing campaign, and threatened to scream and cry until our eardrums burst. Well, not really. But there were a bunch of kids (and parents) that were very angry. Now this blue ice cream is a permanent flavor at the shop. It tastes just like a frozen scoop of freshly spun cotton candy, but believe it or not, we make it with an all-natural flavor extract from Nature's Flavors, along with blue vegetable-based food dye. So this seemingly most unholy flavor of ice cream is actually all natural! Go figure.

1. Prepare Walt's Dream according to the recipe directions. After cooling the base in the ice bath, add the cotton candy extract and stir to combine. Add the food coloring drop by drop to achieve the desired color.

2. Transfer the cooled base to an ice cream maker and churn it according to the manufacturer's instructions.

3. Transfer the ice cream to a storage container. Serve immediately or harden in your freezer for 8 to 12 hours for a more scoopable ice cream.

Give it a twist! Divide the mix in half before you add the coloring and make one half blue and the other half pink. Gently combine for a tie-dye cotton candy swirl.

Black Cow
Float FLOAT!

# BLACK COW FLOAT

If you walked into an ice cream parlor in 1947 and ordered a root beer float, you'd probably end up with something quite different from what you'd get today. The root beer float, also known as a black cow float in the thirties and forties, was root beer mixed with a couple of shots of chocolate syrup and topped with vanilla ice cream. We've attempted to re-create the old black cow experience with this flavor. It's a root beer–flavored ice cream with swirls of milk chocolate.

1. Make the root beer ice cream: Prepare Walt's Dream according to the recipe directions. After cooling the base in the ice bath, add the extracts and stir to combine.

2. Transfer the cooled base to an ice cream maker and churn it according to the manufacturer's instructions.

3. While the ice cream is churning, make the milk chocolate swirl: Place the chocolate in a medium heatproof bowl. In a small saucepan, heat the cream over medium heat until it starts to bubble up. Pour the hot cream over the chocolate and stir gently until the chocolate is completely melted and the mixture is smooth.

4. Transfer the base to a storage container, gently folding in heaping spoonfuls of the milk chocolate swirl as you do, softly lifting and spinning it throughout the ice cream. Be careful not to overmix. Serve immediately or harden in your freezer for 8 to 12 hours for a more scoopable ice cream.

## FOR THE ROOT BEER ICE CREAM:

1 recipe Walt's Dream (page 24)

1 tablespoon root beer extract (see Note)

1 teaspoon vanilla extract

## FOR THE MILK CHOCOLATE SWIRL:

6 ounces (170 g) milk chocolate, chopped

½ cup (120 ml) heavy cream

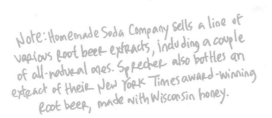

Make a black cow float FLOAT! Add a scoop or two of this ice cream to a glass of root beer with tons of chocolate swirled around inside the glass!

Note: Homemade Soda Company sells a line of various root beer extracts, including a couple of all-natural ones. Sprecher also bottles an extract of their New York Times award-winning root beer, made with Wisconsin honey.

# VANILLA MALTED

1½ pounds (680 g) malted milk balls

1 recipe Walt's Dream (page 24)

½ cup (60 g) malted milk powder

2 teaspoons vanilla extract

"Make it a malted." We love malt at Ample Hills. We add it to our blondie recipe (see page 38), we add it to our chocolate milkshakes, and we even make a peanut butter malted ice cream (see page 112). The rich, milky, wholesome, almost caramel notes of malt powder are a perfect addition to countless other flavors. In this recipe, we add malt powder to vanilla ice cream, along with handfuls of malted milk balls.

1. Place the malted milk balls in the freezer for at least 1 hour.

2. Make the malted ice cream: Prepare Walt's Dream according to the recipe directions. Prior to heating the base, add the malted milk powder and whisk vigorously to combine.

3. Transfer the base to the ice bath, add the vanilla, and stir to combine. Let cool for 15 to 20 minutes. Pour the ice cream base through a wire-mesh strainer into a storage container and place in the refrigerator for 1 to 2 hours, or until completely cool.

4. Transfer the cooled base to an ice cream maker and churn it according to the manufacturer's instructions.

5. While the ice cream is churning, crush the malted milk balls into pieces. At the shop, Brian uses a round metal thingie—he doesn't really know what it's called, or what it's supposed to do, but he thinks of it as his personal malt ball crusher. (Actually, it's a tamping tool for the espresso machine.) You can use any blunt object, such as a wooden mallet or the bottom of a soda bottle. Lay the malted milk balls out on a baking sheet and start whacking away at them, but be careful not to pulverize them too much. We like to keep our pieces fairly large. If you're OK with much smaller pieces, you can throw the malt balls into a food processor for a quick spin.

6. Transfer the cooled base to a storage container, folding in the crushed malted milk balls as you do. Serve immediately or harden in your freezer for 8 to 12 hours for a more scoopable ice cream.

To turn this ice cream flavor (or any flavor, for that matter) into a milkshake, simply combine 3 cups (600 g) ice cream with 1½ cups (360 ml) whole milk in a blender and blend until the mixture reaches the desired consistency. Sip through a straw or eat with a spoon!

# NONNA D'S OATMEAL LACE

Nonna D is Jackie's mom. (The *D* is for Dolores.) The oatmeal cookies we use in this recipe were her specialty. She baked them every Christmas, and the smell of the toasted oats and butter would fill the apartment with warmth and anticipation. She made them as drop cookies, spreading the batter in very thin circles. They were crisp and lacelike, and you could never eat just one. We miss her, and we hope that she would be excited to know her oatmeal cookies live on in this ice cream.

1. Make the brown sugar and cinnamon ice cream: Prepare an ice bath in the sink or in a large heatproof bowl.

2. In a medium saucepan, combine the brown sugar, skim milk powder, cinnamon, and milk. Stir with a hand mixer or whisk until smooth. Make sure the skim milk powder is wholly dissolved into the mixture and that no lumps remain (any remaining sugar granules will dissolve over the heat). Stir in the cream.

3. Clip a candy thermometer to the saucepan and set the pan over medium heat. Cook, stirring often with a rubber spatula and scraping the bottom of the pan to prevent sticking and burning, until the mixture reaches 110°F (45°C), 5 to 10 minutes. Remove the pan from the heat.

4. Place the egg yolks in a medium bowl. While whisking, slowly pour ½ cup (120 ml) of the hot milk mixture into the egg yolks to temper them. Continue to whisk slowly until the mixture is an even color and consistency, then whisk the egg-yolk mixture back into the remaining milk mixture.

(continued)

¾ cup (165 g) packed dark brown sugar

½ cup (60 g) skim milk powder

1¼ teaspoons ground cinnamon

1⅔ cups (400 ml) whole milk

1⅔ cups (400 ml) heavy cream

3 egg yolks

1 teaspoon vanilla extract

FOR THE OATMEAL COOKIES:

Butter for the baking sheet

2⅔ cups (270 g) old-fashioned rolled oats

1 tablespoon + 1 teaspoon all-purpose flour

2⅔ cups (530 g) organic cane sugar

1 teaspoon salt

3 eggs

1 tablespoon + 1 teaspoon vanilla extract

1¼ cups (300 g) unsalted butter, melted

5.  Return the pan to the stovetop over medium heat and continue cooking the mixture, stirring often, until it reaches 165°F (75°C), 5 to 10 minutes more.

6.  Transfer the pan to the prepared ice bath and let cool for 15 to 20 minutes, stirring occasionally. Add the vanilla and stir to combine. Pour the ice cream base through a wire-mesh strainer into a storage container and place in the refrigerator for 1 to 2 hours, or until completely cool.

7.  Make the oatmeal cookies: Preheat the oven to 350°F (175°C). Butter a 12-by-18-inch rimmed baking sheet and line it with parchment paper.

8.  In a large bowl, toss together the oats, flour, sugar, and salt.

9.  In a separate small bowl, whisk the eggs and vanilla together until smooth. Add the butter and whisk to combine. Pour the egg mixture over the oats. Work the dough together with your hands until there are no dry clumps of oats or flour left in the bowl.

10. Spread the mixture in an even layer across the prepared baking sheet (as if you were making a tray of brownies). At the shop, we cook them about ½ inch (12 mm) thick so that we can easily chop them into bite-size pieces. Bake for 20 to 25 minutes, until the top is a deep golden brown. Let cool, then chop the cookies into small pieces and set aside.

11. Transfer the cooled base to an ice cream maker and churn it according to the manufacturer's instructions.

12. Transfer the ice cream to a storage container, folding in the oatmeal cookie pieces as you do. Use as many of the cookie pieces as you want; you won't necessarily need the whole batch. Serve immediately or harden in your freezer for 8 to 12 hours for a more scoopable ice cream.

What CAN YOU FIND at the SODA FOUNTAIN?

☐ flashlight   ☐ lily pad        ☐ chopsticks   ☐ purple goblet
☐ ruler        ☐ Elmer's glue    ☐ ladybug      ☐ baseball
☐ column       ☐ striped straw   ☐ party hat    ☐ book

# NUTTY

for when you feel
like a nut

OUR MERRY ADVENTURERS TRAVEL in the front car of an
elevated subway train, their noses pressed to the
glass, straining to see the great granite stanchion
of the Brooklyn Bridge as they pass underneath. And
now, the city of Manhattan, in the summer of 1947,
stretches out before them. In splendid color, in
real 3-D. "It's gorgeous!" Walt exclaims.

"Why isn't the city in black and white?" PB asks.

Whitty chuckles. He explains to PB that no one
lived in black and white. It was the cameras.

They hop off the train at the first stop in
Manhattan and circle back down toward the river, to
the foot of the Brooklyn Bridge. They stop in front
of a vaulted tunnel, their path blocked by
a chain-link fence. "Here!" Walt yells. He's found
a spot where the fence has been cut and bent back at the bottom.
The three brave travelers climb underneath and make their way down
the darkening tunnel.

"PB, do you smell that?" Whitty asks.

"Peanuts!"

The tunnel opens into a cool, dusty, cavernous cellar. The walls
leap up over their heads, vaulting fifty feet up in the air . . .
And throughout the room, piled from floor to ceiling, are old
wooden crates. Filled with peanuts. Thousands, millions,
gazillions of peanuts.

"They're roasted jumbo salted peanuts. Yummy!" PB stuffs a
handful in his mouth.

"Look, pistachios, too. And walnuts! And pecans!" Whitty shouts.

"But mostly peanuts," PB says proudly.

As Whitty and PB explore the crates of nuts, Walt wanders off on
his own. Something has taken hold of him, pulling him deeper and
deeper into the cellar. There's a wooden table and lots of books.
Someone is living here.

"Whitty, over here!" PB has found another room. As large as the
first, and filled with even more peanuts. A chilly, peanut-y breeze
blows through an open door.

"Oh my gosh!" Walt spots something purple glistening in the soft light. There, on the floor, covered in peanut shells, keeping the door open, letting the peanut-y breeze in from the next room, is the purple goblet!

"I found it!" Walt grabs the goblet, and his eyes go wide with excitement. "I found it!"

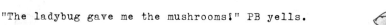

WHAM! The stone door slams shut. *That's strange*, Walt thinks. *The magic goblet was a door stopper?* Whitty and PB race over. Walt cleans out the goblet, and PB scoops his melting Knickerbocker Glory Sundae into it. "Wait," Walt says. "Who goes first?"

"Let's let PB. It's his sundae, after all," Whitty says.

Walt grabs the goblet, holding it tight. "But I don't know. I mean, I found it, right? So . . . "

"The ladybug gave me the mushrooms!" PB yells.

"OK, OK. So maybe we should draw straws," says Walt.

And that's what they do. Whitty draws a short straw. No good. Then PB and Walt draw straws at the same time.

"I win, I win!" Walt says, dancing around gleefully. PB shouts as he tries to grab the goblet. But Walt runs away!

He stumbles into a tower of peanut crates. The crates teeter for a second . . . then come toppling to the ground. CRASH! Whitty and PB try to chase Walt as peanuts spill across the cellar floor. Walt ducks behind another tower of crates. He cradles the goblet in his hands. Whitty and PB grab peanuts and chuck them over the crates at Walt. Peanut fight!

Walt spots an open door in the distance, leading deeper into the cellar. He runs for it! He bobs, weaves, skips, and jumps to avoid the falling peanuts. He slides through the entrance and slams the door shut!

# BUTTER PECAN BRITTLE

This is our take on the classic butter pecan flavor. We leave the butter out of the ice cream itself, instead choosing to let the rich molasses notes of dark brown sugar shine through. Then we make pecan brittle with butter and break that into pieces. Bits of the brittle dissolve into the ice cream, and others stay hard and crunchy.

1. Make the brown sugar ice cream: Prepare an ice bath in the sink or in a large heatproof bowl.

2. In a medium saucepan, combine the brown sugar, skim milk powder, and milk. Stir with a hand mixer or whisk until smooth. Make sure the skim milk powder is wholly dissolved into the mixture and that no lumps remain (any remaining sugar granules will dissolve over the heat). Stir in the cream.

3. Clip a candy thermometer to the saucepan and set the pan over medium heat. Cook, stirring often with a rubber spatula and scraping the bottom of the pan to prevent sticking and burning, until the mixture reaches 110°F (45°C), 5 to 10 minutes. Remove the pan from the heat.

4. Place the egg yolks in a medium bowl. While whisking, slowly pour ½ cup (120 ml) of the hot milk mixture into the egg yolks to temper them. Continue to whisk slowly until the mixture is an even color and consistency, then whisk the egg-yolk mixture back into the remaining milk mixture.

5. Return the pan to the stovetop over medium heat and continue cooking the mixture, stirring often, until it reaches 165°F (75°C), 5 to 10 minutes more.

(continued)

## FOR THE BROWN SUGAR ICE CREAM:

¾ cup (165 g) packed dark brown sugar

½ cup (60 g) skim milk powder

1⅔ cups (400 ml) whole milk

1⅔ cups (400 ml) heavy cream

3 egg yolks

1 teaspoon vanilla extract

## FOR THE PECAN BRITTLE:

Butter for the baking sheet

12 ounces (340 g) pecans, broken into pieces

½ cup (120 ml) golden syrup

1 cup (200 g) organic cane sugar

¾ teaspoon salt

½ cup (120 g) unsalted butter

½ teaspoon baking soda

6. Transfer the pan to the prepared ice bath and let cool for 15 to 20 minutes, stirring occasionally. Add the vanilla and stir to combine. Pour the ice cream base through a wire-mesh strainer into a storage container and place in the refrigerator for 1 to 2 hours, or until completely cool.

7. Make the pecan brittle: Preheat the oven to 275°F (135°C). Butter a 12-by-18-inch rimmed baking sheet and line it with parchment paper.

8. Spread the pecans in a single layer on the baking sheet and toast them until they just begin to change color, about 10 minutes. Let cool, then transfer the pecans to a bowl and set aside. Reserve the prepared baking sheet for the brittle.

9. In a medium saucepan, combine the syrup, sugar, salt, butter, and ¼ cup (60 ml) water. Clip a candy thermometer to the side of the pan and set the pan over medium-high heat. Cook, stirring, until the ingredients are combined and the sugar has dissolved, then continue to cook without stirring until the mixture reaches 305°F (150°C), about 15 minutes.

10. Remove the pan from the heat and stir in the pecans and baking soda. Whisk vigorously for a few moments to combine. Move quickly, as the mixture will begin to set as the temperature drops. Spread the mixture evenly across the prepared baking sheet. Let cool until brittle, about 2 hours.

11. Chop the brittle into bite-size pieces and store in an airtight container in the freezer until ready to use.

12. Transfer the cooled base to an ice cream maker and churn it according to the manufacturer's instructions.

13. Transfer the ice cream to a storage container, folding in the pecan brittle pieces as you do. Use as much of the brittle as you want; you won't necessarily need the whole batch. Serve immediately or harden in your freezer for 8 to 12 hours for a more scoopable ice cream.

One time Christian said, "You butter pecan believe it." To date, it's the best joke he's ever made.

# MAPLE WALNUT BRITTLE

1 recipe maple ice cream
(see page 75)

1 recipe pecan brittle
(see page 99), made with
chopped walnuts instead
of pecans

When we brought Maple
Walnut Brittle back after
a particularly long hia-
tus, a woman called the
shop and asked, "What
are the dimensions of a
tub of ice cream?" She
bought the whole thing
and emptied out her
entire freezer to make
room for the 3-gallon
tub. It was her hus-
band's favorite flavor
and she didn't want to
risk being without it
again.

Here's a flavor that just feels like fall—something to eat on those
pumpkin-picking hayride afternoons. As with our take on butter
pecan, for our version of maple walnut, we make a brittle candy.
The toasted walnuts, butter, and caramelized sugars are magic
together. And the added benefit of making brittle is that the pieces
of walnut don't absorb the liquid from the ice cream and become
soggy. You'll get bright, crunchy bits of nut and butter in every bite.
It's important to find grade B maple syrup for this recipe. It's darker
and richer, so the flavor will stand up to the other ingredients.

1. Prepare the maple ice cream according to the recipe directions.
   Transfer the cooled base to a storage container and refrigerate
   until ready to use.

2. Prepare the pecan brittle according to the recipe directions,
   but substitute walnuts for the chopped pecans.

3. Transfer the cooled base to an ice cream maker and churn it
   according to the manufacturer's instructions.

4. Transfer the ice cream to a storage container,
   folding in the walnut brittle pieces as you do.
   Use as much of the brittle as you want; you
   won't necessarily need the whole batch.
   Serve immediately or harden in your freezer
   for 8 to 12 hours for a more scoopable
   ice cream.

# PISTACHIO SQUARED

It took a long, long, long time for Brian to make a pistachio ice cream. So long, in fact, that when it appeared, the sandwich board outside proclaimed: "Finally!" Growing up, Brian hated nuts. And pistachios most of all. Anything crunchy and nutty was out of the question. He just couldn't bring himself to spend the money or the time on a flavor of ice cream he knew he wouldn't like. But Jackie, Lauren, and one out of every three customers kept badgering him. So eventually, almost two years after opening the shop, he relented. Of course, now it's his new favorite flavor, and to Brian's chagrin there's a whole range of nut flavors at the shop (enough to fill this chapter!). But in Brian's defense, that often happens with cooking. When we use an ingredient ourselves, when we craft something with our own hands, we gain a new appreciation for it. We see the food for the first time. With this recipe, we decided to double up on the creamy nuttiness of pistachios, whisking pistachio paste into the ice cream itself, and adding bits and pieces of homemade brown sugar–pistachio brittle.

## FOR THE PISTACHIO ICE CREAM:

1 recipe Walt's Dream (page 24)

½ cup (120 ml) pistachio paste

## FOR THE PISTACHIO BRITTLE:

Butter for the baking sheet

12 ounces (340 g) pistachios, shelled

½ cup (120 ml) golden syrup

½ cup (100 g) organic cane sugar

½ cup (110 g) packed dark brown sugar

¾ teaspoon salt

½ cup (120 g) unsalted butter

½ teaspoon baking soda

1. Make the pistachio ice cream: Prepare Walt's Dream according to the recipe directions. After cooling the base in the ice bath and straining it, stir in the pistachio paste. Use a hand mixer or whisk to combine until smooth. Transfer the base to a storage container and refrigerate until ready to use.

2. Make the pistachio brittle: Preheat the oven to 275°F (135°C). Butter a 12-by-18-inch rimmed baking sheet and line it with parchment paper. Spread the pistachios over the prepared baking sheet and toast them for 10 minutes, until they just begin to change color. Let cool, then transfer the pistachios to a bowl and set aside. Reserve the prepared baking sheet for the brittle.

(continued)

Finally!

3. In a medium saucepan, combine the syrup, cane sugar, brown sugar, salt, butter, and ¼ cup (60 ml) water. Clip a candy thermometer to the side of the pan and set the pan over medium-high heat. Cook, stirring, until the ingredients are combined and the sugar has dissolved, then continue to cook without stirring until the mixture reaches 305°F (150°C).

4. Remove the pan from the heat and stir in the pistachios and baking soda. Whisk vigorously for a few moments to combine. Move quickly, as the mixture will begin to set as the temperature drops. Spread the mixture evenly across the prepared baking sheet. Let cool until brittle, about 2 hours.

5. Chop the brittle into bite-size pieces and store in an airtight container in the freezer until ready to use.

6. Transfer the cooled base to an ice cream maker and churn it according to the manufacturer's instructions.

7. Transfer the ice cream to a storage container, folding in the pistachio brittle pieces as you do. Use as much of the brittle as you want; you won't necessarily need the whole batch. Serve immediately or harden in your freezer for 8 to 12 hours for a more scoopable ice cream.

# THE PEANUT BUTTER MUNCHIES

3 cups (720 ml) whole milk

1½ cups (about 90 g) mini salted pretzels

¾ cup (150 g) organic cane sugar

½ cup (60 g) skim milk powder

1⅔ cups (400 ml) heavy cream

2 egg yolks

½ cup (125 g) all-natural peanut butter (see Note)

1 recipe munchies mix-in (see page 71)

8 ounces (225 g) Reese's Pieces, chopped

Peanut butter goes with everything! Bananas, marshmallows, malt, chocolate, bacon, jelly . . . At Ample Hills, we've made a dozen different peanut butter flavors. We're constantly searching for the best peanut butter flavor out there, and this might just be it. It's a variation on The Munchies (page 71), but here we add peanut butter to the pretzel-infused base, and replace the M&M's with Reese's Pieces (or peanut butter M&M's, if you prefer).

1. Make the peanut butter–pretzel ice cream: Prepare an ice bath in the sink or in a large heatproof bowl.

2. In a large saucepan, heat the milk over medium-high heat until it starts to steam, 10 to 15 minutes. Remove the pan from the heat and stir in the pretzels. Cover the pan and let the pretzels steep for 20 minutes. Pour the mixture through a wire-mesh strainer into a bowl, pressing on the pretzels to extract as much milk as possible. Don't worry if some of the pretzel "pulp" pushes through into the ice cream. That's totally OK. Return the pretzel-infused milk to the saucepan.

3. Add the sugar and skim milk powder. Stir with a hand mixer or whisk until smooth. Make sure the skim milk powder is wholly dissolved into the mixture and that no lumps remain (any remaining sugar granules will dissolve over the heat). Stir in the cream.

4. Clip a candy thermometer to the saucepan and set the pan over medium heat. Cook, stirring often with a rubber spatula and scraping the bottom of the pan to prevent sticking and burning, until the mixture reaches 110°F (45°C), 5 to 10 minutes. Remove the pan from the heat.

5. Place the egg yolks in a medium bowl. While whisking, slowly pour ½ cup (120 ml) of the hot milk mixture into the egg yolks to temper them. Continue to whisk slowly until the mixture is an even color and consistency, then whisk the egg-yolk mixture back into the remaining milk mixture.

6. Return the pan to the stovetop over medium heat and continue cooking the mixture, stirring often, until it reaches 165°F (75°C), 5 to 10 minutes more. Add the peanut butter and stir until combined.

7. Transfer the pan to the prepared ice bath and let cool for 15 to 20 minutes, stirring occasionally. Pour the ice cream base through a wire-mesh strainer into a storage container and place in the refrigerator for 1 to 2 hours, or until completely cool.

8. While the base cools, prepare the munchies mix-in according to the recipe directions.

9. Transfer the cooled base to an ice cream maker and churn it according to the manufacturer's instructions.

10. Transfer the ice cream to a storage container, folding in the munchies mix-in and Reese's Pieces as you do. Use as much of the mix-in as you want; you won't necessarily need the whole batch. Serve immediately or harden in your freezer for 8 to 12 hours for a more scoopable ice cream.

You can make munchies recipes out of basically any snack food. Experiment—and then invite me over to taste-test!

# PB FLUFF AND STUFF

NAMED BY FACEBOOK FAN BRIAN PAGE

This was one of our early Facebook flavor-naming contest winners. We love to involve our customers in different ways and get ideas from them—sometimes in creating a flavor from scratch (The Creamy Cyclone, page 188), or sometimes in naming a flavor that we've already made. With PB Fluff and Stuff, we had the flavor: an all-natural peanut butter ice cream with swirls of homemade vanilla-bean marshmallow and pieces of peanut butter sandwich cookies. We posted a description on Facebook, and fan Brian Page came up with the name. Extra points for the reference to late sixties kids' show *H. R. Pufnstuf*! Mr. Page won a free pint.

1. Make the peanut butter ice cream: Prepare Walt's Dream according to the recipe directions. Before cooling the base, add the peanut butter and vanilla and whisk vigorously to combine.

2. Transfer the pan to the prepared ice bath and let cool for 15 to 20 minutes. Pour the ice cream base through a wire-mesh strainer into a storage container and place in the refrigerator for 1 to 2 hours, or until completely cool.

3. Prepare the marshmallow fluff according the recipe directions.

4. Transfer the cooled base to an ice cream maker and churn it according to the manufacturer's instructions. While the ice cream is churning, break the cookies into quarters.

5. Transfer the ice cream to a storage container, gently mixing in handfuls of cookies and heaping spoonfuls of marshmallow fluff. Be careful not to overmix, or your marshmallow may dissolve into the ice cream. Serve immediately or harden in your freezer for 8 to 12 hours for a more scoopable ice cream.

## FOR THE PEANUT BUTTER ICE CREAM:

1 recipe Walt's Dream (page 24)

½ cup (125 g) all-natural peanut butter

2 teaspoons vanilla extract

1 recipe Marshmallow Fluff (page 206)

1 (12-ounce/340-g) box or about 25 peanut butter sandwich cookies (see Note)

Another nutty flavor named by a Facebook fan? There's Always Money in the Banana Stand (banana ice cream with flakes of chocolate and peanut brittle), named by Jamie Erika Sanchez to commemorate *Arrested Development*'s return after a seven-year hiatus.

NOTE: We recommend Back to Nature peanut butter sandwich cookies, though other brands (like Nutter-Butter) are also good.

# PB&J

1 recipe peanut butter ice cream (see page 109)

1 cup (240 ml) Concord grape jelly (see Note)

Just like Mom used to make! That is, if Mom had used all-natural peanut butter and organic grape jelly. This flavor always brings childlike smiles to adult faces. But Brian remains unsatisfied. He hasn't yet figured out how to incorporate the sandwich bread into the flavor. Somehow the idea of soggy pieces of Wonder Bread in the ice cream just doesn't cut it. But perhaps there's a way. If you think of one, let us know on Facebook, and we'll be sure to make it very soon.

*Note: We recommend Crofter's organic grape jelly, but please experiment with other brands... and flavors!*

1. Prepare the peanut butter ice cream according to the recipe directions.

2. Transfer the cooled base to an ice cream maker and churn it according to the manufacturer's instructions.

3. Transfer the ice cream to a storage container, gently folding in heaping spoonfuls of the grape jelly as you do, softly lifting and spinning it throughout the ice cream. Be careful not to overmix. Serve immediately or harden in your freezer for 8 to 12 hours for a more scoopable ice cream.

*This is my FAVORITE! But I use strawberry jelly instead.*

# PEANUT BUTTER LOVES COMPANY

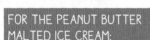

## FOR THE PEANUT BUTTER MALTED ICE CREAM:

¾ cup (165 g) packed dark brown sugar

¼ cup (30 g) skim milk powder

1¾ cups (420 ml) whole milk

1¾ cups (420 ml) heavy cream

2 egg yolks

½ cup (60 g) malted milk powder

½ cup (125 g) all-natural peanut butter

2 teaspoons vanilla extract

## FOR THE SEMISWEET CHOCOLATE SWIRL:

6 ounces (170 g) semisweet chocolate, chopped

¾ cup (180 ml) heavy cream

Often happy to hang out on his own, peanut butter also relishes spending time with friends. Here, he parties hard with robust dark brown sugar, creamy malted milk powder, smooth vanilla, and silky swirls of semisweet chocolate.

1.  Make the peanut butter malted ice cream: Prepare an ice bath in the sink or in a large heatproof bowl.

2.  In a medium saucepan, combine the sugar, skim milk powder, and milk. Stir with a hand mixer or whisk until smooth. Make sure the skim milk powder is wholly dissolved into the mixture and that no lumps remain (any remaining sugar granules will dissolve over the heat). Stir in the cream.

3.  Clip a candy thermometer to the saucepan and set the pan over medium heat. Cook, stirring often with a rubber spatula and scraping the bottom of the pan to prevent sticking and burning, until the mixture reaches 110°F (45°C), 5 to 10 minutes. Remove the pan from the heat.

4.  Place the egg yolks in a medium bowl. While whisking, slowly pour ½ cup (120 ml) of the hot milk mixture into the egg yolks to temper them. Continue to whisk slowly until the mixture is an even color and consistency, then whisk the egg-yolk mixture back into the remaining milk mixture.

5.  Return the pan to the stovetop over medium heat and continue cooking the mixture, stirring often, until it reaches 165°F (75°C), 5 to 10 minutes more.

6.  Remove the pan from the heat and add the malted milk powder, whisking vigorously to combine. Add the peanut butter and vanilla and whisk vigorously until smooth.

7. Transfer the pan to the prepared ice bath and let cool for 15 to 20 minutes, stirring occasionally. Pour the ice cream base through a wire-mesh strainer into a storage container and place in the refrigerator for 1 to 2 hours, or until completely cool.

8. Make the semisweet chocolate swirl: Place the chocolate in a medium heatproof bowl. In a small saucepan, heat the cream over medium heat until it starts to bubble up. Pour the cream over the chocolate and stir gently until the chocolate is completely melted and smooth.

9. Transfer the cooled base to an ice cream maker and churn it according to the manufacturer's instructions.

10. Transfer the ice cream to a storage container, gently folding in heaping spoonfuls of the dark chocolate swirl as you do, softly lifting and spinning it throughout the ice cream. Be careful not to overmix. Serve immediately or harden in your freezer for 8 to 12 hours for a more scoopable ice cream.

MEET THE AMPLOYEES

**BRENT**
"We're All Kids in an Ice Cream Shop!"

**ROSE**
Manager

From: Knoxville, Tennessee
Favorite part of the job: Humoring the chef
Favorite thing to make: Old-fashioned chocolate malts
Weirdest question from a customer: "Is this made with unicorn blood?"

# TIPSY

for when you're
feeling festive

WALT SMILES. HE MADE IT. He's all alone with the goblet. He laughs.
He keeps laughing. Sort of like a bad guy's demonic laugh in a movie.
Then he stops. He digs into the Knickerbocker Glory Sundae. Yum,
yum, yum, yum, yum. When he reaches the last bite, he licks the spoon
clean, holds his breath—and closes his eyes. He can't bear to look.
What if it doesn't—whoa, what's that? Is the goblet getting heavier?
Yes, yes. He peeks. Yes! There's a mountain of fresh ice cream in the
bowl!

Walt shovels the sundae into his mouth again, as if all he wants
to do is get to the bottom of it, to see if it works again. He
takes the last bite. And burps. And again, the Knickerbocker Glory
Sundae reappears.

Walt dances around the room. "It works, it works, it works!"
he yells to the peanuts. But the peanuts don't seem to care.

"Do you hear?! It works, it really works!" Walt charges
a tower of peanuts, toppling it to the ground. Peanuts
coat the floor. One by one, he flips over the crates
of peanuts and pistachios and pecans. Now
the floor is waist-deep in nuts, up to his
big, big belly. He climbs to the top of
another tower of peanuts, and spreads his
arms out as if he were a diver at the
Olympics. He jumps. "Belly flop!!!" he screams
as he sails down into his homemade bouncy house of peanuts and
pistachios and pecans. "Ouch," he says when he lands.

He eats another sundae. And another. Then he climbs back up the
tower of peanuts. He pirouettes into the nuts below. "Wheeeeeeee!"
he screams. Then he pauses to gobble down another Knickerbocker
Glory Sundae. He climbs back up, and this time, he backflips into
the nuts! Then he dives headfirst into the nuts. "Wheeeee!" he
screams again and again. Then he wobbles over to the purple goblet.
He eats another sundae. Now he's stuffed.

He's eaten six sundaes. Or maybe it's seven—he's lost count. He
takes another bite. And another. He can barely lift the spoon to his
mouth. But it's so good. Just one more bite.

Walt mutters, "Just one more, and I'll—"

THWUMP. He passes out with his face in the
goblet of ice cream, the spoon still held
tightly in his hand.

# BOURBON ST.

Inspired by the beautiful, loud, musical city of New Orleans, Bourbon St. combines bourbon vanilla ice cream and pecan pralines. Decadent, grown-up, yet a little bit naughty. The father of one of our scoopers suggested this one and got a free pint for his trouble. (Thanks, Collette's dad!)

1. Make the bourbon vanilla ice cream: Prepare an ice bath in the sink or in a large heatproof bowl.

2. In a medium saucepan, combine the sugar, skim milk powder, and milk. Stir with a hand mixer or whisk until smooth. Make sure the skim milk powder is wholly dissolved into the mixture and that no lumps remain (any remaining sugar granules will dissolve over the heat). Halve the vanilla bean lengthwise and gently scrape the seeds from inside the pod. Add the seeds and pod to the saucepan. Stir in the cream.

3. Clip a candy thermometer to the saucepan and set the pan over medium heat. Cook, stirring often with a rubber spatula and scraping the bottom of the pan to prevent sticking and burning, until the mixture reaches 110°F (45°C), 5 to 10 minutes. Remove the pan from the heat.

4. Place the egg yolks in a medium bowl. While whisking, slowly pour ½ cup (120 ml) of the hot milk mixture into the egg yolks to temper them. Continue to whisk slowly until the mixture is an even color and consistency, then whisk the egg-yolk mixture back into the remaining milk mixture.

5. Return the pan to the stovetop over medium heat and continue cooking the mixture, stirring often, until it reaches 165°F (75°C), 5 to 10 minutes more. Remove the pan from the heat and use a fork to remove and discard the vanilla bean pod.

(continued)

## FOR THE BOURBON VANILLA ICE CREAM:

¾ cup (150 g) organic cane sugar

¾ cup (90 g) skim milk powder

1⅓ cups (315 ml) whole milk

1 vanilla bean

2 cups (480 ml) heavy cream

3 egg yolks

3 tablespoons bourbon (see Note)

1 teaspoon vanilla extract

## FOR THE PECAN PRALINE:

Butter for the baking sheet

10 ounces (280 g) pecans, chopped

1 cup (240 g) unsalted butter

1¼ cups (275 g) packed dark brown sugar

1¼ cups (250 g) organic cane sugar

2 teaspoons vanilla extract

⅓ cup (80 ml) whole milk

⅓ cup (80 ml) heavy cream

NOTE: We use Maker's Mark bourbon at the shop, but feel free to experiment with other varieties.

6. Transfer the pan to the prepared ice bath and let cool for 15 to 20 minutes, stirring occasionally. Add the bourbon and vanilla and stir to combine. Pour the ice cream base through a wire-mesh strainer into a storage container and place in the refrigerator for 1 to 2 hours, or until completely cool.

7. Make the pecan praline: Preheat the oven to 275°F (135°C). Butter a 12-by-18-inch rimmed baking sheet and line it with parchment paper.

8. Spread the pecans evenly across the prepared baking sheet and toast them until they just begin to change color, about 10 minutes. Let cool, then place the pecans in a bowl and set aside. Reserve the prepared baking sheet for the praline.

9. In a large saucepan, combine the butter, brown sugar, cane sugar, vanilla, milk, and cream. Clip a candy thermometer to the side of the pan and set the pan over medium-high heat. Cook, stirring regularly, until the mixture reaches 240°F (115°C). Mixture will bubble vigorously.

10. Remove the pan from the heat and add the pecans. Stir vigorously for 2 minutes. Move quickly, as the mixture will begin to set as the temperature drops. Pour the mixture onto the prepared baking sheet and spread it into an even layer. Let cool completely, then chop the praline into bite-size pieces and set aside.

11. Transfer the cooled base to an ice cream maker and churn it according to the manufacturer's instructions.

12. Transfer the ice cream to a storage container, folding in the pecan praline pieces as you do. Use as much of the praline as you want; you won't necessarily need the whole batch. Serve immediately or harden in your freezer for 8 to 12 hours for a more scoopable ice cream.

# MAKE YOUR OWN DRINK UMBRELLAS CRAFT

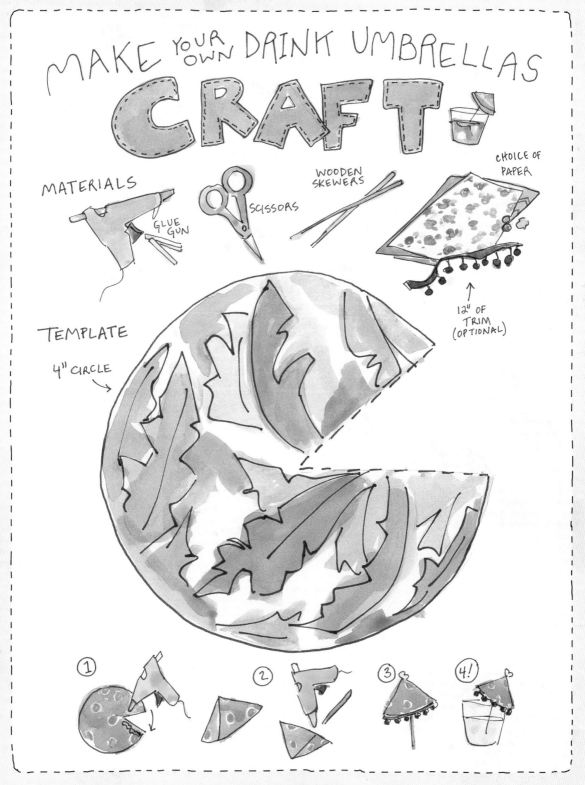

MATERIALS

GLUE GUN

SCISSORS

WOODEN SKEWERS

CHOICE OF PAPER

12" OF TRIM (OPTIONAL)

TEMPLATE

4" CIRCLE

① ② ③ ④!

# DADDY'S SUNDAE

1 recipe bourbon vanilla ice cream (see page 117)

1 recipe brownies (see page 171)

## FOR THE SALTED FUDGE CARAMEL:

1 cup (200 g) organic cane sugar

2 tablespoons unsalted butter

¾ teaspoon salt

1½ cups (360 ml) heavy cream

6 ounces (170 g) semisweet chocolate, chopped

½ teaspoon vanilla extract

Here's an example of how you can combine elements of different recipes or flavors to create something wholly new. You don't always have to reinvent the wheel to create something great. With Daddy's Sundae, we borrow the bourbon vanilla base from Bourbon St. (page 117), add pieces of brownies from Chocolate Three Ways (page 171), and incorporate a swirl of salted fudge caramel to reimagine the idea of an ice cream sundae, just for grown-ups. We introduced this flavor on Father's Day.

1. Prepare the bourbon vanilla ice cream according to the recipe directions. Transfer the cooled base to a storage container and refrigerate until ready to use.

2. Prepare the brownies according to the recipe directions. Let cool completely and break into bite-size pieces. Set aside.

3. Make the salted fudge caramel: In a medium saucepan, heat the sugar over medium-high heat, stirring frequently with a rubber spatula as it melts. When it has melted completely and drips smoothly off the spatula (with no discernable sugar granules), remove the spatula and continue to cook the sugar without stirring. Watch the pan closely—the caramel will turn darker in color. Watch for smoke to rise off the top. When the caramel starts to smoke, count to ten and remove the pan from the heat.

4. Using an oven mitt, carefully add the butter to the pan. It might spatter when it hits the hot caramel, so be careful. Stir the mixture with a rubber spatula until the butter has melted and the mixture is smooth and combined. Add the salt. Slowly pour in the cream—it will bubble up, but you must continue to stir it as you pour, so the cream incorporates smoothly into the caramel. Be careful!

(continued)

YAWP!

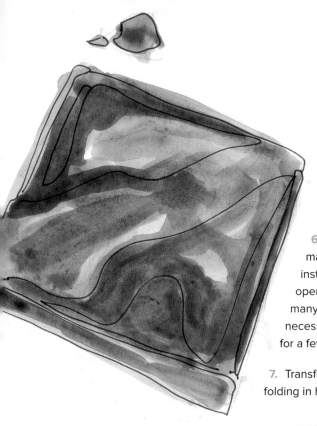

5. Add the chocolate and stir until it has melted and the mixture is smooth. Add the vanilla and stir to combine. Set aside to cool.

6. Transfer the cooled base to an ice cream maker and churn it according to the manufacturer's instructions. When the ice cream is nearly finished, open the lid and add the brownie pieces. Use as many of the brownie pieces as you want; you won't necessarily need the whole batch. Continue churning for a few minutes more.

7. Transfer the ice cream to a storage container, gently folding in heaping spoonfuls of the salted fudge caramel as you do, softly lifting and spinning it throughout the ice cream. Be careful not to overmix. Serve immediately or harden in your freezer for 8 to 12 hours for a more scoopable ice cream.

MEET THE AMPLOYEES

JASON
"I Don't Know, Can You?"
SMITH
Head of Special Events

From: Bronx, New York
Extracurricular activities: Father, husband, student, and all-around good guy
Favorite thing to make: The Icy Spicy Milkshake—equal parts Mexican Hot Chocolate and Peppermint Pattie
Craziest request from a customer: "Just shovel the ice cream into my mouth."

# THE DUDE

At Ample Hills, we'd like to think that if The Dude from *The Big Lebowski* staggered into the shop, he'd approve of his namesake flavor. His drink of choice, a White Russian, consists of vodka and coffee liqueur. We make it by steeping freshly ground coffee beans in milk and adding Brooklyn Republic Vodka. The Dude abides.

2 cups (480 ml) whole milk

¾ cup (75 g) coarsely ground coffee beans

¾ cup (150 g) organic cane sugar

½ cup plus 3 tablespoons (80 g) skim milk powder

2 cups (480 ml) heavy cream

3 egg yolks

¼ cup (60 ml) vodka

1. Prepare an ice bath in the sink or in a large heatproof bowl.

2. In a large saucepan, heat the milk over medium-high heat until it starts to steam, 10 to 15 minutes. Remove the pan from the heat and stir in the coffee. Cover the pan and let the coffee steep for 10 minutes. Pour the mixture through a cheesecloth-lined wire-mesh strainer into a bowl. Return the coffee-infused milk to the saucepan.

3. Add the sugar and skim milk powder. Stir with a hand mixer or whisk until smooth. Make sure the skim milk powder is wholly dissolved into the mixture and that no lumps remain (any remaining sugar granules will dissolve over the heat). Stir in the cream.

4. Clip a candy thermometer to the saucepan and set the pan over medium heat. Cook, stirring often with a rubber spatula and scraping the bottom of the pan to prevent sticking and burning, until the mixture reaches 110°F (45°C), 5 to 10 minutes. Remove the pan from the heat.

5. Place the egg yolks in a medium bowl. While whisking, slowly pour ½ cup (120 ml) of the hot milk mixture into the egg yolks to temper them. Continue to whisk slowly until the mixture is an even color and consistency, then whisk the egg-yolk mixture back into the remaining milk mixture.

(continued)

The Dude
abides.

6. Return the pan to the stovetop over medium heat and continue cooking the mixture, stirring often, until it reaches 165°F (75°C), 5 to 10 minutes more. Add the vodka and stir to combine.

7. Transfer the pan to the prepared ice bath and let cool for 15 to 20 minutes, stirring occasionally. Pour the ice cream base through a wire-mesh strainer into a storage container and place in the refrigerator for 1 to 2 hours, or until completely cool.

8. Transfer the cooled base to an ice cream maker and churn it according to the manufacturer's instructions.

9. Transfer the ice cream to a storage container. Serve immediately or harden in your freezer for 8 to 12 hours for a more scoopable ice cream.

# DRUNKEN THANKSGIVING

## FOR THE PUMPKIN-BOURBON ICE CREAM:

¾ cup (165 g) packed dark brown sugar

½ cup plus 3 tablespoons (85 g) skim milk powder

1 cup (240 ml) whole milk

2⅓ cups (560 ml) heavy cream

1 cup (240 ml) unsweetened pumpkin puree

4 egg yolks

¼ cup (60 ml) bourbon

1 teaspoon vanilla extract

½ teaspoon ground cinnamon

¼ teaspoon ground ginger

¼ teaspoon ground nutmeg

⅛ teaspoon ground cloves

A slice of pumpkin pie with whipped cream, a tumbler of bourbon on the rocks, and a chewy molasses-ginger cookie—mash 'em up, toss 'em together, and you have a Drunken Thanksgiving. That's what we love about ice cream: the endless flavor possibilities. Just consider your favorite meal, your favorite drink, or your favorite dessert—we promise you there's an ice cream flavor lurking nearby.

1. Make the pumpkin-bourbon ice cream: Prepare an ice bath in the sink or in a large heatproof bowl.

2. In a medium saucepan, combine the sugar, skim milk powder, and milk. Stir with a hand mixer or whisk until smooth. Make sure the skim milk powder is wholly dissolved into the mixture and that no lumps remain (any remaining sugar granules will dissolve over the heat). Add the cream. Use a cheesecloth to squeeze any excess water out of the pumpkin puree; add the puree. Whisk to combine.

3. Clip a candy thermometer to the saucepan and set the pan over medium heat. Cook, stirring often with a rubber spatula and scraping the bottom of the pan to prevent sticking and burning, until the mixture reaches 110°F (45°C), 5 to 10 minutes. Remove the pan from the heat.

4. Place the egg yolks in a medium bowl. While whisking, slowly pour ½ cup (120 ml) of the hot milk mixture into the egg yolks to temper them. Continue to whisk slowly until the mixture is an even color and consistency, then whisk the egg-yolk mixture back into the remaining milk mixture.

5.  Return the pan to the stovetop over medium heat and continue cooking the mixture, stirring often, until it reaches 165°F (75°C), 5 to 10 minutes more. Remove the pan from the heat and add the bourbon, vanilla, cinnamon, ginger, nutmeg, and cloves. Whisk to combine.

6.  Transfer the pan to the prepared ice bath and let cool for 15 to 20 minutes, stirring occasionally. Pour the ice cream base through a wire-mesh strainer into a storage container and place in the refrigerator for 1 to 2 hours, or until completely cool.

7.  Make the molasses cookies: Preheat the oven to 350°F (175°C). Butter a 12-by-18-inch baking sheet and line it with parchment paper.

8.  In a medium bowl, whisk together the flour, baking soda, cinnamon, cloves, ginger, and salt.

9.  In the bowl of a stand mixer fitted with the paddle attachment, beat the butter, cane sugar, and brown sugar on medium speed until combined. Add the eggs and molasses and continue beating until combined. Reduce the mixer speed to low and add the dry ingredients, 1 cup (about 100 g) at a time, beating until just combined after each addition before adding the next.

10. Sprinkle some flour on your hands and press the dough into an even layer, approximately ¼ inch (6 mm) thick, on the prepared baking sheet. Bake for 10 to 12 minutes or until a knife inserted in the center comes out clean. Let cool completely, then chop the cookie layer into bite-size pieces.

11. Transfer the cooled base to an ice cream maker and churn it according to the manufacturer's instructions.

12. Transfer the ice cream to a storage container, folding in the molasses cookie pieces as you do. Use as many of the cookie pieces as you want; you won't necessarily need the whole batch. Serve immediately or harden in your freezer for 8 to 12 hours for a more scoopable ice cream.

Butter for the baking sheet

3 cups (375 g) all-purpose flour, plus extra for your hands

2 teaspoons baking soda

1½ teaspoons ground cinnamon

1 teaspoon ground cloves

1 teaspoon ground ginger

1 teaspoon salt

1 cup (240 g) unsalted butter

1 cup (200 g) organic cane sugar

½ cup (110 g) packed dark brown sugar

2 eggs

½ cup (120 ml) molasses

Tired of bringing a boring pumpkin pie to the Thanksgiving table? Make an Ice Cream Cake (page 214) using this flavor. You'll be the most popular guest there!

# EGGNOG

¾ cup (150 g) organic cane sugar

½ cup (60 g) skim milk powder

1⅔ cups (400 ml) whole milk

1⅔ cups (400 ml) heavy cream

10 egg yolks

2 tablespoons rum

2 teaspoon vanilla extract

½ teaspoon nutmeg

⅛ teaspoon cinnamon

Winter is obviously a slower time at the shop, but you'd be surprised at the number of devoted cold-weather customers. Some people actually prefer ice cream in the winter. In addition to serving our Hot Chocolate (page 207) at the shop, we offer seasonal ice cream flavors that are best enjoyed in a sweater, and nothing quite captures the feeling of Christmastime like a cool glass of eggnog. In this recipe we quadruple the number of egg yolks in our basic sweet cream recipe and add nutmeg, cinnamon, and a splash of rum. The resulting ice cream is simultaneously spicy, boozy, and eggy. Just don't check your cholesterol.

1. Prepare an ice bath in the sink or in a large heatproof bowl.

2. In a medium saucepan, combine the sugar, skim milk powder, and milk. Stir with a hand mixer or whisk until smooth. Make sure the skim milk powder is wholly dissolved into the mixture and that no lumps remain (any remaining sugar granules will dissolve over the heat). Stir in the cream.

3. Clip a candy thermometer to the saucepan and set the pan over medium heat. Cook, stirring often with a rubber spatula and scraping the bottom of the pan to prevent sticking and burning, until the mixture reaches 110°F (45°C), 5 to 10 minutes. Remove the pan from the heat.

4. Place the egg yolks in a medium bowl. While whisking, slowly pour ½ cup (120 ml) of the hot milk mixture into the egg yolks to temper them. Continue to whisk slowly until the mixture is an even color and consistency, then whisk the egg-yolk mixture back into the remaining milk mixture.

5. Return the pan to the stovetop over medium heat and continue cooking the mixture, stirring often, until it reaches 165°F (75°C), 5 to 10 minutes more.

6. Remove the pan from the heat and add the rum, vanilla, nutmeg, and cinnamon. Whisk to combine. Transfer the pan to the prepared ice bath and let cool for 15 to 20 minutes, stirring occasionally. Pour the ice cream base through a wire-mesh strainer into a storage container and place in the refrigerator for 1 to 2 hours, or until completely cool.

7. Transfer the cooled base to an ice cream maker and churn it according to the manufacturer's instructions.

8. Transfer the ice cream to a storage container. Serve immediately or harden in your freezer for 8 to 12 hours for a more scoopable ice cream.

We made another great seasonal flavor for Hanukkah called Festival of Lights, using cream cheese ice cream (see page 63) and chopped-up raspberry rugelach.

Another idea? Try this recipe with bourbon instead. Or leave out the alcohol for a teetotaler version.

# STOUT AND PRETZELS

1 recipe Dark Chocolate (page 36)

¾ cup (180 ml) Guinness beer

1½ cups (110 g) chocolate-covered pretzels, chopped

From the early days, this was one of our favorites at the shop. Beer and chocolate go great together. We experimented with a number of different beers, but kept coming back to the richness of Guinness. And the darker the chocolate, the better, too. Toss in some salty chocolate-covered pretzels, and you've got yourself a trip to the corner pub on a Friday night.

1. Prepare Dark Chocolate according to the recipe directions. Once the base reaches 165°F (75°C), remove the pan from the heat and mix in the cooled chocolate paste, adding the Guinness at the same time. Transfer the pan to an ice bath and let cool for 15 to 20 minutes. Pour the ice cream base through a wire-mesh strainer into a storage container and place in the refrigerator for 1 to 2 hours, or until completely cool.

2. Transfer the cooled base to an ice cream maker and churn it according to the manufacturer's instructions.

3. Transfer the ice cream to a storage container, folding in the pretzels as you do. Serve immediately or harden in your freezer for 8 to 12 hours for a more scoopable ice cream.

> On St. Patrick's Day, we substitute toffee-covered peanuts for the pretzels and call it Lucky Nuts!

Cin Cin!

# LEMON SKY
## (DAIRY-FREE)

Brian and Jackie vacationed along the Amalfi coast in Italy some years ago, and they still remember sipping ice-cold limoncello at every sidewalk café and restaurant. Limoncello is a lemon liqueur that captures the bright, sweet, velvety tang of fresh lemons. Here we pair it with ginger puree for a light, billowy cloud of lemon-ginger sorbet. But because it's a water-based sorbet, there's no milk fat to hold the spinning air and give it body. We add egg whites for this reason (think of whipping whites into a meringue, and you get the idea). They give this sorbet its unique texture.

1¼ cups (300 ml) lemon juice

1 cup (200 g) organic cane sugar

2 tablespoons corn syrup

4 egg whites

1 teaspoon ginger puree

⅓ cup (80 ml) limoncello

1. Prepare an ice bath in the sink or in a large heatproof bowl.

2. In a medium saucepan, combine the lemon juice, sugar, corn syrup, egg whites, ginger puree, and 2½ cups (600 ml) water. Whisk vigorously until smooth.

3. Clip a candy thermometer to the saucepan and set the pan over medium heat. Cook, stirring regularly, until the mixture reaches 165°F (75°C). Transfer the pan to the prepared ice bath and let cool for 15 to 20 minutes. Stir in the limoncello. Pour the sorbet base through a wire-mesh strainer into a storage container and place in the refrigerator for 1 to 2 hours, or until completely cool.

4. Transfer the cooled base to an ice cream maker and churn it according to the manufacturer's instructions.

5. Transfer the sorbet to a storage container. Serve immediately or harden in your freezer for 8 to 12 hours for a more scoopable sorbet.

> When they were left to their own devices (i.e., when Brian was away), Lauren and Adam replaced all the water in the Lemon Sky recipe with champagne, added some grapefruit, and made the most expensive flavor to date—I'll Drink To That!— for the 2013 New Year.

For grown-ups only: Spice up your gin and tonic with a dollop of Lemon Sky.

# SLUGGISH

for when you need
a kick in the pants

WALT'S ALARM CLOCK BUZZES. Actually, it clucks like a chicken. Bok-bok-bok—

He smacks it against the wall. It's five o'clock in the morning. The sun's not even up. He drags himself out of bed and staggers to the kitchen. He grabs a triple shot of espresso. Gulps it down. Picks up his briefcase and heads to the garage. He can't decide which car to drive. There are three identical fancy convertible sports cars. One is green. One is red. And one is purple. Eeny, meeny, miny, moe. He picks the purple one. Off to work!

He pulls into his private parking spot in front of a large neon sign of himself diving into a ginormous purple bowl of ice cream. The neon sign reads "Wacky Walt's Ice Cream."

Walt storms through the factory, testing the ice cream as it moves down the assembly line. He barks at two chickens working on the line, yelling at them to stop talking and move faster. "Time is money, and if you're wasting time, it's like you're taking my money. And you don't want to take my money, do you, chickens?! Let's go, go, go!"

At the end of the assembly line, putting lids on pints of ice cream, is PB.

"Good morning, Mr. Walt," PB says nervously.

But Walt ignores him and grabs a pint. "What's this? I didn't approve this!"

PB says, "It's our new flavor, sir. Mexican Hot Chocolate."

Walt tastes it. "It's too dense. It's too dark. Too much chocolate. Too expensive!"

"But Mr. Walt, it was your idea. And people really like it."

"Make the chocolate lighter. Milk chocolate is cheaper. And make it less heavy. More air! The secret ingredient is air. Sell more air! That's our motto. Sell more air!"

Walt heads to his office. As he enters, he hangs a "Do Not Disturb" sign on his door.

He sits down at his desk. He's pooped. He thinks, *Running an ice cream empire is hard work, and no one appreciates everything that*

*I do. They're all out there lollygagging and having fun, and I'm the one who has to pay all the bills. Ugh. I need to take a nap.*

And so he does.

An hour later, Whitty kicks Walt. "Wake up! The freezers are broken. There's an ice cream flood in the kitchen. People are swimming in the ice cream! Wake up, Mr. Walt!"

"Oh no!" Walt wakes up. But it's not Whitty kicking him. It's an old man with a long white beard. And Walt isn't in his ice cream office. He's underneath the Brooklyn Bridge. In the cellar. And he's lying face down in melted ice cream and peanut shells.

Walt feels like he's glued to the floor.

"Get up, get up! You can't sleep on the floor. Look what you've done to my peanuts!"

Walt sits up. Rubs his weary eyes. Everything is blurry, and his head hurts.

"They need air to breathe. You took the doorstop! You took it and you killed the breeze. The nuts need air to breathe."

"I'm sorry," Walt mumbles. "Who are you?"

"I'm the keeper of the peanuts. And the pistachios, and pecans, too. But mostly the peanuts."

The old man picks up the purple goblet and thrusts it in Walt's face. "You took this. You took the doorstop! Do you have any idea what it means?"

"It's a magic goblet."

"It lets the peanuts breathe. My precious little peanuts. I banish you! Get out, get out. Go now! The peanuts don't want you here."

Walt stumbles over the peanut shells and hurries out of the cellar.

He steps into the blinding sunlight. Walt shields his eyes and staggers down the street, banging into a trash can. "Whitty? PB?" he cries. "Where are you? Come back!"

# COOKIE AU LAIT

1 (12-ounce/340-g) box or about 25 sandwich cookies, such as Back to Nature

FOR THE COFFEE ICE CREAM:

2 cups (480 ml) whole milk

¾ cup (75 g) coarsely ground coffee beans

¾ cup (150 g) organic cane sugar

½ cup (60 g) skim milk powder

1⅔ cup (400 ml) heavy cream

3 egg yolks

Make an affogato—a shot of hot espresso over a scoop of ice cream! Now that's a kick in the pants!

Coffee ice cream with pieces of all-natural sandwich cookies. Seems so simple. In fact, when Lauren suggested this flavor to Brian, he said, "Eh . . . sounds boring. We have coffee ice cream, and Sweet Cream and Cookies (page 40). Do we really need to combine them?" The answer: oh, yes. The dark, savory, almost bitter notes of coffee are transformed with each sweet and comforting bite of cookie.

1.  Place 6 cookies in the freezer for 1 hour. Transfer the cookies to a small food processor and process them into crumbs. Or, for slightly more fun, place the cookies in a zip-top bag and pound them with your fist! Set this cookie "powder" aside.

2.  Make the coffee ice cream: Prepare an ice bath in the sink or in a large heatproof bowl.

3.  In a medium saucepan, heat the milk over medium-high heat until it starts to steam, 10 to 15 minutes. Remove the pan from the heat and stir in the coffee. Cover the pan and let the coffee steep for 10 minutes. Pour the mixture through a cheesecloth-lined wire-mesh strainer into a bowl. Return the coffee-infused milk to the saucepan.

4.  Add the sugar and skim milk powder. Stir with a hand mixer or whisk until smooth. Make sure the skim milk powder is wholly dissolved into the mixture and that no lumps remain. Stir in the cream.

5.  Clip a candy thermometer to the saucepan and set the pan over medium heat. Cook, stirring often with a rubber spatula and scraping the bottom of the pan to prevent sticking and burning, until the mixture reaches 110°F (45°C), 5 to 10 minutes. Remove the pan from the heat.

6.  Place the egg yolks in a medium bowl. While whisking, slowly pour ½ cup (120 ml) of the hot milk mixture into the egg yolks to temper them. Continue to whisk slowly until the mixture is an

Macha Flake
(page 140)

Cookie
au Lait
(Left)

even color and consistency, then whisk the egg yolk mixture
back into the remaining milk mixture.

7.  Return the pan to the stovetop over medium heat and continue
    cooking the mixture, stirring often, until it reaches 165°F (75°C),
    5 to 10 minutes more. Transfer the pan to the prepared ice bath
    and let cool for 15 to 20 minutes.

8.  Pour the ice cream base through a wire-mesh strainer into a
    storage container and place in the refrigerator for 1 to 2 hours,
    or until completely cool. Stir in the cookie "powder" and churn
    the mixture according to the manufacturer's instructions. Break
    the remaining cookies into quarters.

9.  Transfer the ice cream to a storage container, folding in the
    cookie pieces as you do. Serve immediately or harden in your
    freezer for 8 to 12 hours for a more scoopable ice cream.

# MOCHA FLAKE

## FOR THE MOCHA ICE CREAM:

1 recipe chocolate paste
(see page 36)

2 cups (480 ml) whole milk

1 cup (100 g) coarsely ground
coffee beans

¾ cup (150 g) organic cane
sugar

½ cup (60 g) skim milk
powder

1⅔ cups (400 ml) heavy
cream

2 egg yolks

## FOR THE CHOCOLATE FLAKE:

6 ounces (170 g) bittersweet
chocolate, chopped

2 tablespoons vegetable
shortening (see Note)

Note: We use Spectrum brand
non-hydrogenated vegetable
shortening, but any brand will
work in a pinch. (The vegetable
shortening keeps the chocolate
flakes from becoming little
chocolate bricks in your ice cream.)

Mocha Flake contains almost twice as much coffee as our regular
coffee ice cream. That's because we need the extra coffee to
stand up to the robust flavor of the dark chocolate. But watch out:
It also means there's a *lot* of caffeine per scoop! It's a real pick-me-
up. Also, we add bits of dark chocolate flakes at the end to give
the ice cream a slightly chewy texture and an added hit of flavor.

1. Make the mocha ice cream: Prepare the chocolate paste
   according to the recipe directions. Set aside to cool.

2. Prepare an ice bath in the sink or in a large heatproof bowl.

3. In a large saucepan, heat the milk over medium-high heat until
   it starts to steam, 10 to 15 minutes. Remove the pan from the
   heat, add the ground coffee beans, and stir. Cover the pan and
   let the coffee steep for 10 minutes. Pour the mixture through a
   cheesecloth-lined wire-mesh strainer into a bowl. You should
   have about 1½ cups of coffee milk. If you're short, press down
   on the ground beans to squeeze more milk out of them. Return
   the coffee-infused milk to the saucepan.

4. Add the sugar and skim milk powder. Stir with a hand mixer or
   whisk until smooth. Make sure the skim milk powder is wholly
   dissolved into the mixture and that no lumps remain (any
   remaining sugar granules will dissolve over the heat). Stir in the
   cream.

5. Clip a candy thermometer to the saucepan and set the pan over
   medium heat. Cook, stirring often with a rubber spatula and
   scraping the bottom of the pan to prevent sticking and burning,
   until the mixture reaches 110°F (45°C), 5 to 10 minutes. Remove
   the pan from the heat.

6. Place the egg yolks in a medium bowl. While whisking, slowly pour ½ cup (120 ml) of the hot milk mixture into the egg yolks to temper them. Continue to whisk slowly until the mixture is an even color and consistency, then whisk the egg-yolk mixture back into the remaining milk mixture.

7. Return the pan to the stovetop over medium heat and continue cooking the mixture, stirring often, until it reaches 165°F (75°C), 5 to 10 minutes more. Remove the pan from the heat and add the chocolate paste and coffee extract. Whisk to combine.

8. Transfer the pan to the prepared ice bath and let cool for 15 to 20 minutes, stirring occasionally. Pour the ice cream base through a wire-mesh strainer into a storage container and place in the refrigerator for 1 to 2 hours, or until completely cool.

9. Make the chocolate flake: In a small saucepan, combine the chocolate and shortening and heat over very low heat, stirring constantly to prevent burning.

10. Transfer the cooled base to an ice cream maker and churn it according to the manufacturer's instructions. Midway through the freezing process, open the lid, and, with the machine running, gently pour the chocolate flake mixture into the ice cream. As the ice cream spins, the liquid chocolate will freeze and break apart into little flakes. If your ice cream maker prevents you from churning with the lid off, don't worry; there's a work-around. Finish churning the ice cream, then transfer it to a storage container, drizzling the melted chocolate into the ice cream as you do. Use a spoon to quickly stir and break the chocolate into flakes.

11. Serve immediately or harden in your freezer for 8 to 12 hours for a more scoopable ice cream.

# WACKY WALT'S BINGO

| | | | | |
|---|---|---|---|---|
| COFFEE | PIZZA | FLOUR | HERBS | PAPER TOWELS |
| PENCIL | LIGHT BULB | CACTUS | APPLE | DOG |
| CAT | LETTUCE | FREE SPACE | DOG BOWL | SOUP |
| MILK | FLOWERS | FISH | CHAIR | DISH TOWEL |
| GRAPES | CEREAL | BIRD | CLOCK | TABLESPOON |

Do you see any of these objects around your kitchen? Take turns with a friend or sibling until you get BINGO: 5 across, down, or diagonal.

| | | | | |
|---|---|---|---|---|
| PEANUTS | GLOBE | ORANGE JUICE | FAN | LIGHT BULB |
| ICE CREAM SCOOPER | BANANAS | CEREAL | PUMPKIN | CLOCK |
| CACTUS | MUG | FREE SPACE | TEA KETTLE | SODA CAN |
| OVEN MITT | TEASPOON | MILK | PINT OF ICE CREAM | CAT |
| CRACKERS | KITCHEN TIMER | SPONGE | COFFEE | LETTUCE |

* USE COFFEE BEANS AS BINGO PIECES

# MEXICAN HOT CHOCOLATE

**1 recipe Dark Chocolate (page 36)**

**1 teaspoon ground red-pepper flakes**

**2 teaspoons ground cinnamon**

The name tends to confuse people: *Wait, is it hot or cold? Is it a drink? Or is it melted ice cream? Can I still get it on a cone if it's hot?* It's not that kind of hot! It's a spicy-hot dark chocolate ice cream. You get warm and soothing cinnamon notes with a sharp kick of red-pepper flakes at the end, driving you back again and again for one more cold-hot-cold-hot bite of ice cream.

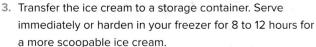

1. Prepare Dark Chocolate according to the recipe directions, adding the red-pepper flakes and cinnamon when you add the chocolate paste.

2. Transfer the cooled base to an ice cream maker and churn it according to the manufacturer's instructions.

3. Transfer the ice cream to a storage container. Serve immediately or harden in your freezer for 8 to 12 hours for a more scoopable ice cream.

# SALTED CRACK CARAMEL

Once upon a time, in the years and months before we opened the shop, Brian remembers making this flavor for friends and family. There were many who said this was the only thing he needed to make in order to be successful. There were others who strongly disliked it and warned Brian against selling it at all. "It's burnt. It's bitter. People will hate it." To this day, the flavor continues to polarize. But enough people love it to make it far and away our most popular flavor. Once, on the weekend after Salted Crack Caramel won *New York* magazine's Crackiest Crack Food in Town award, nearly 25 percent of all our sales came from this one flavor. That's out of twenty-four flavors! There are days in the summer when we sell fifteen gallons of Salted Crack. If it were just salted caramel ice cream, it might not be as popular. But we add Deb's crack cookies to the ice cream—extremely sweet and addictive, they are the perfect counterpoint to the salty bitterness of the burnt-caramel ice cream.

1. Make the salted caramel ice cream: Prepare an ice bath in the sink or in a large heatproof bowl.

2. In a medium saucepan, heat the sugar over medium-high heat, stirring frequently with a rubber spatula as it melts. When it has melted completely and drips smoothly off the spatula (with no discernable sugar granules), remove the spatula and continue to cook the sugar without stirring. Watch the pan closely—the caramel will turn darker in color. Watch for smoke to rise off the top. When the caramel starts to smoke, count to ten and remove the pan from the heat.

(continued)

## FOR THE SALTED CARAMEL ICE CREAM:

1½ cups (300 g) organic cane sugar

¼ cup (60 g) unsalted butter

1 teaspoon salt

1 cup (240 ml) heavy cream

2 cups (480 ml) whole milk

6 egg yolks

## FOR DEB'S CRACK COOKIES:

Butter for the baking sheet

45 saltine crackers

¾ cup (180 g) unsalted butter

1 cup (200 g) organic cane sugar

1 teaspoon vanilla extract

10 ounces (280 g) milk chocolate, chopped

3. Using an oven mitt, carefully add the butter to the pan. It might spatter when it hits the hot caramel, so be careful. Stir the mixture with a rubber spatula until the butter has melted and the mixture is smooth and combined. Add the salt. Slowly pour in the cream—it will bubble up, but you must continue to stir it as you pour, so the cream incorporates smoothly into the caramel. Be careful! Add the milk and stir to combine.

4. Clip a candy thermometer to the saucepan and return the pan to the heat. Cook, stirring often with a rubber spatula and scraping the bottom of the pan to prevent sticking and burning, until the mixture reaches 110°F (45°C), 5 to 10 minutes. Remove the pan from the heat.

5. Place the egg yolks in a medium bowl. While whisking, slowly pour ½ cup (120 ml) of the hot milk mixture into the egg yolks to temper them. Continue to whisk slowly until the mixture is an even color and consistency, then whisk the egg-yolk mixture back into the remaining milk mixture.

6. Return the pan to the stovetop over medium heat and continue cooking the mixture, stirring often, until it reaches 165°F (75°C), 5 to 10 minutes more.

7. Transfer the pan to the prepared ice bath and let cool for 15 to 20 minutes, stirring occasionally. Pour the ice cream base through a wire-mesh strainer into a storage container and place in the refrigerator for 1 to 2 hours, or until completely cool.

8. Make Deb's crack cookies: Preheat the oven to 350°F (175°C). Butter a 12-by-18-inch baking sheet and line it with parchment paper.

9. Spread the crackers out in even rows in a single layer on the prepared baking sheet.

10. In a medium saucepan, melt the butter and sugar over medium-high heat, whisking occasionally to combine. When the butter and sugar start to bubble up, remove the pan from the heat and whisk in the vanilla.

11. Gently pour the butter mixture over the crackers and use a spatula to spread it evenly. Bake for 15 to 20 minutes or until the sugar has caramelized, turning light brown in color.

(continued)

Use Deb's crack cookies to make ice cream sandwiches. Smear about ½ inch (12 mm) of the ice cream of your choice over one cookie, top with another, and freeze overnight. They're messy, but amazing!

12. Remove the baking sheet from the oven and sprinkle the chocolate over the crackers. Wait a few moments for the chocolate to begin to melt, then use a spatula to gently spread the chocolate over the crackers in an even layer.

13. Let the crack cookies cool. Refrigerate for 1 hour, then chop the cookies into bite-size pieces and set aside.

14. Transfer the cooled base to an ice cream maker and churn it according to the manufacturer's instructions.

15. Transfer the ice cream to a storage container, folding in the crack cookie pieces as you do. Use as many of the cookie pieces as you want; you won't necessarily need the whole batch. Serve immediately or harden in your freezer for 8 to 12 hours for a more scoopable ice cream.

## DISCOVERING THE CRACK COOKIES

Brian and Jackie first encountered Deb's crack cookies (and each other) while working as teachers, just out of college. They taught at an alternative school, mainly designed for students suspended for weapon possession. They would often meet up for lunch (or just a brief period of sanity) in the guidance counselor's office, which is how they met Debbie, the guidance counselor.

Not only would Debbie listen to them vent their frustrations about the school, but she would also bring them food. And when they were really feeling down, Debbie would bring in her chocolate cracker cookies, aptly referred to as the crack cookies because they were insanely addictive.

She dressed them in many forms. She added crushed peppermint candies for the Christmas vibe, substituted matzoh for saltines during Passover, coconut flakes just because, and white chocolate when she really wanted to sweeten things up. The variations are endless, really.

Brian and Jackie knew they had to use them somehow, someday, in some flavor of ice cream. And this is how Salted Crack Caramel came to be. Thank you, Debbie!

# PEPPERMINT PATTIE

This flavor is Brian's personal ode to summertime at the movies. Brian and his best friend, Robb, used to down large boxes of Junior Mints while catching every new sci-fi movie at the Cineplex. In the shop's early days, Brian bought cases of Junior Mints to chop into this flavor. The problem? Chopping Junior Mints is a pain. The inside oozes out, and all the pieces stick together. Plus, they're just not strong enough. They're good at the movies, when you're watching aliens destroy the Earth, but not good enough for our ice cream. So we made our own. It's important to use peppermint oil for this recipe. It's super-concentrated (and will make you cry for hours if you get it near your eyes), so just a few drops will give you an arctic blast of cool mint. A scoop of Peppermint Pattie is the perfect antidote to a sweltering summer day.

1. Make the peppermint ice cream: Prepare Walt's Dream according to the recipe directions. After cooling the base in the ice bath, add the vanilla and peppermint extracts and stir to combine. Pour the ice cream base through a wire-mesh strainer into a storage container and place in the refrigerator for 1 to 2 hours, or until completely cool.

2. Make the peppermint patties: Butter a 12-by-18-inch rimmed baking sheet and line it with parchment paper.

3. In the bowl of a stand mixer, beat the butter and 3 tablespoons of the vegetable shortening together on high speed, until light and fluffy. Add the cream, peppermint oil, and vanilla and mix on medium speed until smooth and well combined.

4. In a small saucepan, melt the white chocolate over very low heat, stirring regularly to prevent it from burning.

(continued)

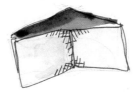

## FOR THE PEPPERMINT ICE CREAM:

1 recipe Walt's Dream (page 24)

½ teaspoon vanilla extract

1½ teaspoons peppermint extract

## FOR THE PEPPERMINT PATTIES:

Butter for the baking sheet

3 tablespoons unsalted butter

5 tablespoons (65 g) vegetable shortening

½ cup (120 ml) heavy cream

½ teaspoon peppermint oil

¾ teaspoon vanilla extract

6 ounces (170 g) white chocolate

5 cups (500 g) confectioners' sugar

12 ounces (340 g) bittersweet chocolate

## FOR THE DARK CHOCOLATE SWIRL:

8 ounces (225 g) bittersweet chocolate, chopped

¾ cup (180 ml) heavy cream

5.  Add the white chocolate to the mixer bowl and beat on medium speed until combined.

6.  With the mixer on low speed, add the confectioners' sugar 1 cup (100 g) at a time, increasing the mixer speed after each addition. Mix on high speed until smooth and well combined. Be sure to keep mixing until any lumps of sugar are gone.

7.  Spread the peppermint mixture in an even layer, no more than ¼ inch (6 mm) thick, on the prepared baking sheet. It will be incredibly sticky and difficult to work with. Coat your hands in powdered sugar, and work the mixture evenly across the sheet, smoothing it out as much as possible. Refrigerate for 30 minutes.

8.  Meanwhile, in a small saucepan, melt the bittersweet chocolate and the remaining 2 tablespoons of vegetable shortening over low heat. Pour over the chilled sheet of peppermint pattie mix, tilting the pan to coat it evenly. Return the baking sheet to the refrigerator for at least 1 hour more, until the chocolate coating is firm. Chop the peppermint pattie into small pieces and set aside.

9.  Transfer the cooled base to an ice cream maker and churn it according to the manufacturer's instructions.

10. While the ice cream is churning, make the dark chocolate swirl: Place the chocolate in a medium heatproof bowl. In a small saucepan, heat the cream over medium heat until it starts to bubble up. Pour the hot cream over the chocolate and stir gently until the chocolate is completely melted and smooth.

11. When the ice cream is almost finished churning, open the lid of the ice cream maker and add the pieces of peppermint pattie. Use as much of the pattie as you want; you won't necessarily need the whole batch. Continue churning for a few minutes more.

12. Transfer the ice cream to a storage container, gently folding in heaping spoonfuls of the dark chocolate swirl as you do, softly lifting and spinning it throughout the ice cream. Be careful not to overmix. Serve immediately or harden in your freezer for 8 to 12 hours for a more scoopable ice cream.

## KIDS' CORNER

The white chocolate mixture used to make the peppermint patties is like fragrant and edible Play-Doh (finally!). Invite your kids to make characters or just smush the mixture into the tray. After freezing the mixture, you can coat your creations in chocolate and devour them. It won't last very long outside the freezer, but it is delicious.

# HEARTBROKEN

for when ice cream is your only friend

WALT'S HEAD THROBS, and he can't remember what happened before he passed out. He remembers the goblet, and the Knickerbocker Glory Sundae, but he can't remember how he got—oh, wait—oh, no . . . He wipes a tear from his eye, as the memories flood back.

He remembers how he took the goblet from his friends, how mean he was, how selfish.

Now his head *really* hurts.

Walt sees water up ahead. He steps across splintered planks of wood as he reaches the very edge of Manhattan, the East River stretching out in front of him, Brooklyn beyond.

Above him, up, up, up, a universe away, are countless people, walking and driving and talking and biking across the Brooklyn Bridge. He hears their distant voices and feels the thrum of engines, the energy and life, and it makes him feel very sad and very alone.

Then, in the distance, halfway across the bridge, walking back to Brooklyn, he spots a very tiny pig. It's PB, and next to him, holding his hand, is Whitty.

"Whitty! PB! I'm here! Don't leave me! Over here! Whitteeeeeeee! PBeeeeeeeeeee!"

But Whitty and PB are quickly swallowed up in the crowd.

Walt jumps into the East River! The cool water washes away the pain in his head. He swims fast and strong. He has to make it back to Brooklyn. He has to find his friends.

As he swims, Walt rehearses all of the ways he'll say he's sorry.

Walt pulls himself ashore. He watches the streams of people walking off the bridge.

But he's missed them. They could be anywhere. All through the afternoon and into the night, Walt searches for his friends. At 3 a.m. he gives up and buys a pint of chocolate peanut butter ice cream. He wanders home to eat and sleep and feel sorry for himself.

But when he gets home, his key doesn't work. He rings the bell. A bleary-eyed ostrich comes to the door. "What are you doing in my house?" Walt demands.

The ostrich screams. "Excuse me?! What are you doing on *my* front stoop?"

"Now, listen here, birdbrain, I've had a bad day, and I need to watch TV and go to sleep."

"TV? What's are you talking about?"

"Oh, of course. I forgot! You're right, I forgot to eat the mushroom."

"OK, eat your mushroom, crazy cow, but just do it on someone else's front stoop, or I'll call the police."

The ostrich slams the door in Walt's face. "Just wait," Walt shouts. "I'll be back, and you'll be gone. And I'll have a TV. And you won't. And then you'll be sorry."

Walt takes a bite of the mushroom. He sails up through time. He spins and twirls up above the building tops. He watches as Brooklyn changes beneath him. In the distance, he sees Ebbets Field demolished. Other buildings rise and fall. Then, in a flash, Barclays Center appears, and Walt knows he's back.

THWUNK! He's home. Back on his own stoop. His key works. The ostrich is gone.

Walt enters his lonely apartment. He pops in an old VHS tape labeled "At park with Whitty and PB." He grabs the pint of chocolate peanut butter ice cream and collapses on the couch. On the TV, Walt tries to nap while PB bounces up and down on his belly. The camera zooms in on Walt's face. There's a soft little smile there as he nods off. But with each pounce on his belly, Walt's eyes flit open. Whitty narrates the video: "Can he do it, folks? Wait—yes! Success! Walt's done it. He's fallen asleep while acting as a porcine trampoline! Well done, sir, well done."

On the couch, Walt sighs and takes a bite of the ice cream.

Maybe it's because the ice cream is sixty years old. Or maybe it's because he's all alone. Either way, it just doesn't taste the same without his friends. But Walt takes another bite anyway. And another. It's cold. Smooth. It's not that bad, actually. Sorta kinda good.

He spoons more of the ice cream into his mouth, longing for his friends on the TV.

# CAUGHT IN THE RAIN
## THE PIÑA COLADA SORBET (DAIRY-FREE)

2 cups (480 ml) unsweetened coconut milk

2 cups (480 ml) all-natural pineapple juice

¾ cup (150 g) organic cane sugar

¼ cup (60 ml) fresh lime juice

4 egg whites

3 tablespoons corn syrup

2 tablespoons rum

"If you like piña coladas, and getting caught in the rain . . . If you like making love at midnight . . . write to me and escape." Rupert Holmes wrote these goofy, beautiful lyrics in the late seventies about a couple in a broken marriage looking for a fresh connection, who end up finding it in each other. Our sorbet captures the comforting sweetness of this classic love song between creamy coconut milk and sweet pineapple juice.

1. Prepare an ice bath in the sink or in a large heatproof bowl.

2. In a medium saucepan, combine the coconut milk, pineapple juice, sugar, lime juice, egg whites, and corn syrup and whisk vigorously until smooth.

3. Clip a candy thermometer to the saucepan and set the pan over medium heat. Cook, stirring regularly, until the mixture reaches 165°F (75°C).

4. Transfer the pan to the prepared ice bath and let cool for 15 to 20 minutes, stirring occasionally. Add the rum and stir to combine.

5. Transfer the cooled base to an ice cream maker and churn it according to the manufacturer's instructions.

6. Transfer the sorbet to a storage container. Serve immediately or harden in your freezer for 8 to 12 hours for a more scoopable sorbet.

GROWN-UPS ONLY: blend this SORBET with more RUM. Add a drink umbrella and serve poolside.

If you like
piña coladas...

Serves one
lonely heart.

# OOEY GOOEY BUTTER CAKE

This flavor is second only to Salted Crack Caramel (page 147) in popularity. Nothing is sweeter, more sinful, or more of a guilty pleasure than Ooey Gooey Butter Cake. It's exactly the indulgence you need to mend a broken heart. Originally a St. Louis tradition, the cake is something Brian first had during summers at Trout Lake in upstate New York. Hilda, the grand matron of Trout Lake, made the cakes for potluck dinners. Brian asked her for the recipe, but she said no. After sneaking into her cabin but failing to wrestle the recipe from Hilda's wiry hands, Brian remembered Google, and went to work. A couple of seconds later, he had found hundreds of recipes. As with many dishes, there really isn't a secret to good ooey gooey butter cake, except the quality of the ingredients you use. We use an organic yellow cake mix, real vanilla beans, and European butter with a high fat content. Then we add cream cheese to the ice cream to highlight the gooey, cheesy qualities of the cake.

1 recipe cream cheese ice cream (see page 63)

### FOR THE OOEY GOOEY BUTTER CAKE:

Butter for the baking pan

1 cup (240 g) unsalted butter

1 vanilla bean

1 package yellow cake mix

3 eggs

8 ounces (225 g) cream cheese

1 teaspoon vanilla extract

1 pound (455 g) confectioners' sugar

1. Prepare the cream cheese ice cream according to the recipe directions. Transfer the cooled base to a storage container and refrigerate until ready to use.

2. Make the ooey gooey butter cake: Preheat the oven to 350°F (175°C). Butter a 9-by-13-inch baking pan and line it with parchment paper.

3. Place ½ cup (120 g) of the butter in a small saucepan. Halve the vanilla bean lengthwise and scrape out the seeds. Add the seeds and pod to the pan with the butter and cook over low heat until the butter has melted. Use a fork to remove and discard the pod.

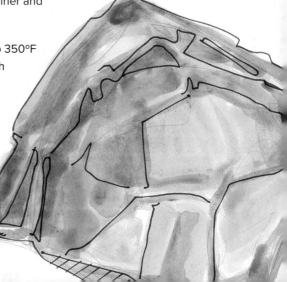

(continued)

4. In the bowl of a stand mixer fitted with the paddle attachment, beat together the cake mix, 1 egg, and the melted butter on medium speed until just combined. The batter will be thick and doughlike. Spread it evenly across the prepared baking pan.

5. In a small saucepan, melt the remaining ½ cup (120 g) butter. In the clean bowl of a stand mixer fitted with a clean paddle attachment, beat the cream cheese on high speed until smooth. Add the remaining 2 eggs, vanilla, and melted butter and beat on medium speed until combined. Add the confectioners' sugar and beat on low until combined. Now increase speed to high and beat until completely smooth.

6. Pour the cream cheese mixture over the cake batter. Bake for 45 minutes to an hour, until the top has browned slightly, and the cake is no longer jiggly in the middle. Let the cake cool completely, then chop it into bite-size pieces.

7. Transfer the cooled base to an ice cream maker and churn it according to the manufacturer's instructions.

8. Transfer the ice cream to a storage container, folding in the pieces of ooey gooey butter cake as you do. Use as much of the cake as you want; you won't necessarily need the whole batch. Serve immediately or harden in your freezer for 8 to 12 hours for a more scoopable ice cream.

MEET THE AMPLOYEES

**MAX**

*"Lemme Know If You Wanna Try Something, Darlin'"*

**KELLY**

Resident Funny Man

From: Brooklyn, New York

Extracurricular activity: Struggling philanthropist, successful nocturnal creature

If I could invent a flavor: Jameson coffee ice cream with chocolate ooey gooey cake and crack cookies. It would be called Sweet Tooth's Revenge.

Best (or most repeated) joke: When people ask to try Salted Crack Caramel, "Are you a cop?"

# CHOCOLATE PEANUT BUTTER

Nothing comforts a broken heart better than this soothing combination of dark chocolate ice cream and creamy peanut butter. Peanut butter is a strong flavor, and we like to swirl in lots and lots of it, so it's important to make the chocolate dark and rich. That way, it can stand up to the peanut butter and be an equal dance partner.

1 recipe Dark Chocolate (page 36)

1 cup (240 ml) heavy cream

2 teaspoons golden syrup

¼ cup (50 g) organic cane sugar

1 cup (250 g) all-natural peanut butter

1 teaspoon vanilla extract

1. Prepare Dark Chocolate according to the recipe directions. Transfer the cooled base to a storage container and refrigerate until ready to use.

2. Make the peanut butter swirl: In a medium saucepan, combine the cream, syrup, and sugar and cook over low heat, stirring occasionally, until the sugar granules have dissolved, but not a moment longer. Remove the pan from the heat and add the peanut butter and vanilla. Whisk until smooth.

3. Transfer the cooled base to an ice cream maker and churn it according to the manufacturer's instructions.

4. Transfer the ice cream to a storage container, gently folding in heaping spoonfuls of the peanut butter mixture as you do, softly lifting and spinning it throughout the ice cream. Be careful not to overmix. Serve immediately or harden in your freezer for 8 to 12 hours for a more scoopable ice cream.

* THERE ARE TEN!

# BAKED/UNBAKED

1 recipe Vanilla Bean
(page 34)

Butter for the baking sheet

2 cups (250 g) all-purpose
flour, plus extra for your
hands

½ teaspoon baking soda

1¼ cups (300 g) unsalted
butter, at room temperature

1 cup (200 g) organic cane
sugar

½ cup (120 ml) golden syrup

1 teaspoon salt

2 tablespoons vanilla extract

12 ounces (340 g) semisweet
chocolate, chopped

Originated by Ben & Jerry's more than twenty years ago, cookie
dough has become a staple at ice cream parlors across the
country. It's a comfort flavor that captures the guilty pleasure of
impulsively eating raw chocolate chip cookie dough when you
just don't have the patience to bake it. But why choose between
cookie dough and actual cookies? At Ample Hills, we feature both
baked and unbaked cookie dough pieces in our pure Vanilla Bean
ice cream. The only difference in the two cookie recipes below is
that we leave out the eggs in the unbaked version.

1. Prepare Vanilla Bean according to the recipe directions.
   Transfer the cooled base to a storage container and refrigerate
   until ready to use.

2. Make the chocolate chip cookie dough: Butter a 12-by-18-inch
   rimmed baking sheet and line it with parchment paper.

3. In a small bowl, whisk together the flour and baking soda.

4. In the bowl of a stand mixer fitted with the paddle attachment,
   beat together the butter and sugar on medium speed until
   light and fluffy. Add the syrup, salt, and vanilla and beat until
   combined. Reduce the speed to low and add the flour mixture,
   beating until just combined. Stir in the chocolate pieces by
   hand.

5. Dip your hands in flour and spread the sticky batter in an
   even layer, ¼ inch (6 mm) thick, on the prepared baking sheet.
   Freeze until solid, about 1 hour. Chop the dough into bite-size
   pieces and freeze them until ready to use.

6. Make the chocolate chip cookies: Preheat the oven to 350°F
   (175°C). Butter a 12-by-18-inch rimmed baking sheet and line it
   with parchment paper.

7. In a small bowl, whisk together the flour, salt, and baking soda.

8. In the bowl of a stand mixer fitted with the paddle attachment, beat together the butter and sugar on medium speed until light and fluffy. Add the syrup, vanilla, and eggs and beat until combined. Reduce the speed to low and add the flour mixture, beating until just combined. Stir in the chocolate pieces by hand.

9. Dip your hands in flour, and spread the sticky batter in an even layer, ¼ inch (6 mm) thick, on the prepared baking sheet. Bake for 10 to 12 minutes, until the top browns and a knife inserted into the cookie comes out without crumbs. Let cool, then chop the cookie into bite-size pieces.

10. In a large bowl, toss together the pieces of unbaked cookie dough and baked cookies.

11. Transfer the cooled base to an ice cream maker and churn it according to the manufacturer's instructions.

12. Transfer the ice cream to a storage container, folding in the cookie-dough and baked-cookie pieces as you do. Use as many of the cookie pieces as you want; you won't necessarily need the whole batch. Serve immediately or harden in your freezer for 8 to 12 hours for a more scoopable ice cream.

In the summer of 2013, we had an outpost at Brooklyn Bridge Park and made flavors for each movie they showed in the park that summer. The inaugural movie, *Ferris Bueller's Day Off*, inspired our flavor Playing Cookie: vanilla ice cream with cookie dough and sandwich cookies, a fun variation of this recipe, especially if you don't feel like baking.

## FOR THE CHOCOLATE CHIP COOKIES:

Butter for the baking sheet

2 cups (280 g) all-purpose flour

1 teaspoon salt

½ teaspoon baking soda

1¼ cups (300 g) unsalted butter, at room temperature

1 cup (200 g) organic cane sugar

½ cup (120 ml) golden syrup

2 tablespoons vanilla extract

2 eggs

12 ounces (340 g) semisweet chocolate, chopped

# TOFFEE BAR CRUNCH

1 recipe Vanilla Bean
(page 34)

FOR THE TOFFEE:

Butter for the baking sheet

2 cups plus 2 tablespoons
(510 g) unsalted butter

2¼ cups (450 g) organic
cane sugar

½ cup (110 g) packed dark
brown sugar

1½ teaspoons salt

½ teaspoon baking soda

2½ teaspoons vanilla extract

6 ounces (170 g) semisweet
chocolate, chopped

As a teenager, Brian absolutely loved Ben & Jerry's. They were
an inspiration for so much of Ample Hills. Brian's favorite flavor
was Heath Bar Crunch: pure vanilla ice cream with giant chunks
of Heath bars. Most ice cream shops have a toffee bar crunch, but
Heath (or Toffee) Bar Crunch is one of those flavors that proves
the value of making things from scratch. We don't mess with the
basics. No Ample Hills twist here. No point in tampering with that
perfect combination of vanilla ice cream and chocolate-covered
pieces of butter toffee. But the simple formula is transformed into
magic with a few short steps: Make your own vanilla ice cream
with real vanilla beans, and make your own butter toffee using real
chocolate, sugar, and butter. It's worth the effort.

1.  Prepare Vanilla Bean according to the recipe directions.
    Transfer the cooled base to a storage container and refrigerate
    until ready to use.

2.  Make the toffee: Butter a 12-by-18-inch baking sheet and line it
    with parchment paper.

3.  In a medium saucepan, combine the butter, cane sugar, brown
    sugar, salt, and ¼ cup (60 ml) water. Cook over medium
    heat, stirring regularly, until the butter is melted and all of the
    ingredients are combined.

4.  Clip a candy thermometer to the saucepan and continue
    heating the mix, without stirring, until it reaches 305°F (150°C).
    Remove the pan from the heat and whisk in the baking soda
    and vanilla. Be careful: The vanilla might spatter.

(continued)

5. Spread the toffee in an even layer, ¼ inch (6 mm) thick, on the prepared baking sheet.

6. Sprinkle the chocolate pieces over the toffee. Wait a few moments for the chocolate to begin to melt, then use a rubber spatula to spread the chocolate evenly across the toffee. Let cool. Refrigerate the toffee until brittle, about 1 hour, then chop it into bite-size pieces and set aside.

7. Transfer the cooled base to an ice cream maker and churn it according to the manufacturer's instructions.

8. Transfer the ice cream to a storage container, folding in the toffee pieces as you do. Use as much of the toffee as you want; you won't necessarily need the whole batch. Serve immediately or harden in your freezer for 8 to 12 hours for a more scoopable ice cream.

MEET THE AMPLOYEES

BRIAN
"The Best Thing I've Ever Made"
SMITH

Oh Captain, My Captain

From: Boca Raton, Florida
Extracurricular activities: Father, husband, and wearer of Muppets T-shirts
Favorite part of the job: Eating ice cream for breakfast
Craziest thing a customer has ever said: "You're like the Mickey Mantle of ice cream."

# CHOCOLATE THREE WAYS

This was one of our first flavors, dating back to the days before we opened the shop, when we sold ice cream out of a pushcart. Three kinds of chocolate come together in perfect harmony in this decadent way to get your chocolate fix: milk chocolate ice cream, dark chocolate brownies, and a white chocolate swirl. It's critical to use the best quality chocolate you can find, so each of the flavors bursts through.

1. Prepare the chocolate milk ice cream according to the recipe directions. Transfer the cooled base to a storage container and refrigerate until ready to use.

2. Make the white chocolate swirl: Place the white chocolate in a medium heatproof bowl. In a small saucepan, heat the cream over medium heat until it starts to bubble up. Pour the hot cream over the white chocolate and stir gently until the white chocolate is completely melted and smooth.

3. Make the brownies: Preheat the oven to 350°F (175°C). Butter a 12-by-18-inch rimmed baking sheet and line it with parchment paper.

4. In a medium saucepan, combine the chocolate, butter, and shortening. Heat on low until melted, stirring regularly to prevent the chocolate from burning. Remove from the heat and set aside.

5. In a small bowl, whisk together the flour, cocoa powder, baking powder, and salt.

(continued)

1 recipe chocolate milk ice cream (see page 43)

## FOR THE WHITE CHOCOLATE SWIRL:

8 ounces (225 g) white chocolate, chopped

¼ cup (60 ml) heavy cream

## FOR THE BROWNIES:

Butter for the baking sheet

14 ounces (400 g) semi-sweet chocolate

¾ cup (180 g) unsalted butter

3 tablespoons (40 g) vegetable shortening

¾ cup (90 g) all-purpose flour

¼ cup (20 g) cocoa powder

½ teaspoon baking powder

½ teaspoon salt

5 eggs

1⅔ cups (330 g) organic cane sugar

¼ cup (60 ml) golden syrup

2 teaspoons vanilla extract

Oopsies!

6. In another small bowl, whisk the eggs together with the sugar, syrup, and vanilla. Pour into the pan with the melted chocolate. Whisk to combine. Add the dry ingredients and whisk.

7. Spread the brownie batter on the prepared sheet and bake for 12 to 15 minutes, until the surface starts to crack and flake. The brownies will still be a little gooey, but shouldn't be wet and jiggly. Let them cool completely, then chop them into bite-size pieces. Set aside.

MEET THE AMPLOYEES

VANESSA
"Golf Ball- or Baseball-Size Scoop?"
DE RIGGS
The Original Scooper

From: Brooklyn, New York
Extracurricular activity: Aspiring clinical psychologist
Favorite part of the job: Meeting awesome new and regular customers!
Craziest thing a customer has ever said: "Do you know how many calories are in each ice cream?" (A lot.)

8. Transfer the cooled base to an ice cream maker and churn it according to the manufacturer's instructions. When the ice cream is almost finished, open the lid and add the brownies. Use as many of the brownie pieces as you want; you won't necessarily need the whole batch. Continue churning for a few minutes more.

9. Transfer the ice cream to a storage container, gently folding in heaping spoonfuls of the white chocolate swirl as you do, softly lifting and spinning it throughout the ice cream. Be careful not to overmix. Serve immediately or harden in your freezer for 8 to 12 hours for a more scoopable ice cream.

8

# INSPIRED

for when you
are channeling your
creative juices

WALT SLEEPS ON THE COUCH. The half-eaten pint of chocolate peanut butter ice cream is perched on his belly, melting. It lifts up with each breath, almost tipping, and falls back down. Up, down. The ice cream soup sloshes over the edge and spills down Walt's belly.

He jumps up, awake, and the ice cream splashes all over the couch.

"Yuck!" Walt yells. "Ugh. Why does that keep happening to me?!"

After a quick shower, Walt calls Whitty. But Whitty's not there. Walt leaves a voice message. "Hi, Whitty. Hi, PB. How are you? I'm just...I'm calling because...Well, you know. That was pretty neat, huh? To see Brooklyn in the olden days? Um, call me."

After a minute, Walt calls back and leaves another message.

"I forgot to say something. I'm sorry. I guess I didn't act very nice. I hope you guys ate your mushrooms. Call me."

Walt waits five minutes. He calls Whitty back.

"Hello. It's me again. Forgot to say I'm home. So call me at home. OK?"

Walt waits ten minutes.

"Hello, it's moo again. Tell PB I got some chocolate peanut butter ice cream. I think he'd like it. Well, actually, it's kind of melted. So never mind. But, yeah, so...Call me."

Walt counts to ten, then calls Whitty back. But he can't think of anything else to say.

He hangs up.

He looks around his apartment. He doesn't know what to do now. He checks the time. It's eight o'clock in the morning. *I guess it's time for breakfast*, he thinks. *Ice cream on a waffle, just like PB would have if he were here for a sleepover. That'll make me feel better.*

Walt opens the freezer. Oh, no. No more ice cream.

He sinks to the ground and cries. No friends. No ice cream. He's lost everything.

He bangs his head back into the refrigerator door.

And that's when a box of ice cream cones slips off the top of the freezer and smacks Walt in the head.

"Ouch." He picks up the box of cones. There's a picture of three kids licking their gigantic scoops of ice cream. They're smiling and happy together.

"That's it!" Walt jumps up. "I'll make ice cream. And I'll invite Whitty and PB to come help make it. And eat it. That way, when it's all gone, we can just make some more. We can always just make some more. And we won't need the magic goblet!"

Except Walt doesn't know how to make ice cream. But that's OK. He can learn, right?

Over the next hours and days and weeks, Walt buries himself in ice cream books. He learns about milk and cream and cows. (Well, he learns *more* about cows, like how we can help make them happy so they make the best milk possible.) He learns about the chemistry of ice cream. He learns about ice crystals, and how to do battle with them! And he learns about the secret ingredient in all ice cream: air! (Which helps make ice cream poofy and smooth and light, like a cloud.)

Then Walt sits down to write.

He writes an apology and an invitation to his friends. And he writes the story of their adventure back in time. Then he writes a list of recipes, including all of Whitty's and PB's favorites. Sunday Brunch, for example. And The Creamy Cyclone.

He titles his cookbook adventure story with one very simple and magical word:

MORE

# FOUR MORE YEARS

¾ cup (150 g) organic cane sugar

¾ cup (90 g) skim milk powder

1⅓ cups (315 ml) whole milk

2⅓ cups (560 ml) heavy cream

4 egg yolks

½ cup (120 ml) Ommegang Witte beer

1 recipe honeycomb candy (see page 44)

As the Obama v. Romney election neared, we knew we needed a pair of flavors to go head-to-head. For Romney, inspiration came easy. We made a very expensive flavor: Rom Raisin, rum-soaked raisins in a rum-and-vanilla-bean ice cream. Good, but not popular at all. For Obama, it took a while to come up with a fitting flavor. Then a customer reminded us that Obama keeps honeybees at the White House—and a microbrewery! So we came up with a sweet cream and Ommegang beer ice cream with pieces of our homemade honeycomb candy.

1. Make the beer ice cream: Prepare an ice bath in the sink or in a large heatproof bowl.

2. In a medium saucepan, combine the sugar, skim milk powder, and milk. Stir with a hand mixer or whisk until smooth. Make sure the skim milk powder is wholly dissolved into the mixture and that no lumps remain (any remaining sugar granules will dissolve over the heat). Stir in the cream.

3. Clip a candy thermometer to the saucepan and set the pan over medium heat. Cook, stirring often with a rubber spatula and scraping the bottom of the pan to prevent sticking and burning, until the mixture reaches 110°F (45°C), 5 to 10 minutes. Remove the pan from the heat.

4. Place the egg yolks in a medium bowl. While whisking, slowly pour ½ cup (120 ml) of the hot milk mixture into the egg yolks to temper them. Continue to whisk slowly until the mixture is an even color and consistency, then whisk the egg-yolk mixture back into the remaining milk mixture.

5. Return the pan to the stovetop over medium heat and continue cooking the mixture, stirring often, until it reaches 165°F (75°C), 5 to 10 minutes more. Remove the pan from the heat and stir in the beer.

(continued)

6. Transfer the pan to the prepared ice bath and let cool for 15 to 20 minutes, stirring occasionally. Pour the ice cream base through a wire-mesh strainer into a storage container and place in the refrigerator for 1 to 2 hours, or until completely cool.

7. Prepare the honeycomb candy according to the recipe directions.

8. Transfer the cooled base to an ice cream maker and churn it according to the manufacturer's instructions.

9. Transfer the ice cream to a storage container, folding in the honeycomb candy pieces as you do. Use as much of the candy as you want; you won't necessarily need the whole batch. Serve immediately or harden in your freezer for 8 to 12 hours for a more scoopable ice cream.

Adding beer to ice cream can be tricky. Choose a beer that highlights the flavors of the ice cream—here, we chose a beer with fruit and honey flavors to complement the sweetness of the ice cream and honeycomb candy, but you can try whichever you like! We try to avoid hops-heavy beers, like IPAs, and choose beers that are naturally sweet, like Hefeweizen.

# AUTUMN IN NEW YORK
## (DAIRY-FREE)

While Sinatra croons about autumn in the big city, with its "glimmering crowds in canyons of steel," our sorbet celebrates autumn in upstate New York, with its rolling hills of apple orchards and its farms filled with towering maple trees. To make this sorbet, we mull apple cider with maple syrup and a blend of warm spices.

4 cups (960 ml) apple cider

½ cup (120 ml) Grade B maple syrup

4 cinnamon sticks

2 tablespoons lemon juice

4 egg whites

2 teaspoons whole cloves

1 tablespoon golden syrup

½ teaspoon ground ginger

2 tablespoons Amaretto liqueur

1. Prepare an ice bath in the sink or in a large heatproof bowl.

2. In a medium saucepan, combine the cider, maple syrup, cinnamon sticks, lemon juice, egg whites, cloves, golden syrup, and ginger. Whisk to combine.

3. Clip a candy thermometer to the saucepan and set the pan over medium heat. Cook until the mixture reaches 165°F (75°C). Remove the pan from the heat and cover. Set aside for 10 minutes to allow the cinnamon sticks and cloves to steep. Strain out the cinnamon sticks and cloves.

4. Transfer the pan to the prepared ice bath and let cool for 15 to 20 minutes. Add the Amaretto.

5. Transfer the cooled base to an ice cream maker and churn it according to the manufacturer's instructions.

6. Transfer the sorbet to a storage container. Serve immediately or harden in your freezer for 8 to 12 hours for a more scoopable sorbet.

# THE ELVIS IMPERSONATOR

1 recipe banana ice cream
(see page 56)

## FOR THE CANDIED BACON:

Butter for the baking sheet

1 pound (455 g) bacon

2 cups (440 g) packed dark
brown sugar

## FOR THE PEANUT BUTTER SWIRL:

1 cup (240 ml) heavy cream

2 teaspoons honey

¼ cup (50 g) organic cane
sugar

1 cup (250 g) peanut butter

1 tablespoon vanilla extract

Inspiration for ice cream flavors can come from just about anywhere: Walks down the aisles of the grocery store, of course. Flipping through the pages of cookbooks, yes. Even visiting other ice cream shops! But inspiration can also come from our favorite movies, TV shows, and novels. Once we made a *Breaking Bad* flavor called Heisenberry and a *Muppets* flavor called Miss Piggy a la Mode! This is our ode to The King and one of his favorite foods: a peanut butter, banana, and bacon sandwich. We've incorporated the banana into an ice cream base and added swirls of honey-sweetened peanut butter and pieces of candied bacon.

1. Prepare the banana ice cream according to the recipe directions. Transfer the cooled base to a storage container and refrigerate until ready to use.

2. Make the candied bacon: Preheat the oven to 375°F (190°C). Butter a 12-by-18-inch rimmed baking sheet and line it with parchment paper. Set a rack over the baking sheet.

3. In a medium bowl, toss the bacon in the brown sugar. Lay strips of bacon in rows on the rack over the prepared baking sheet. Bake for 20 minutes, or until the sugar melts and bubbles up and the bacon starts to brown at the edges. Let cool. Freeze for 1 hour, then chop or break the bacon into small bits and pieces.

4. Make the peanut butter swirl: In a medium saucepan, combine the cream, honey, and sugar. Cook over low heat until the sugar granules have dissolved, but no longer. Remove the pan from the heat and add the peanut butter and vanilla. Whisk until smooth. Set aside.

Want to pay the ultimate homage to The King? Make a banana split with this flavor.

5. Transfer the cooled base to an ice cream maker and churn it according to the manufacturer's instructions. When the ice cream is almost finished, open the lid and add the candied bacon pieces. Use as much of the bacon as you want; you won't necessarily need the whole batch. Continue churning for a few minutes more.

6. Transfer the ice cream to a storage container, gently folding in heaping spoonfuls of the peanut butter swirl as you do, softly lifting and spinning it throughout the ice cream. Be careful not to overmix. Serve immediately or harden in your freezer for 8 to 12 hours for a more scoopable ice cream.

# SUNDAY BRUNCH

There's no better meal than Sunday brunch. You get to convince yourself that you're eating a meal (and not dessert) as you load up on French toast. If you feel inspired, consider replacing the French toast with other brunch favorites such as waffles or pancakes.

1. Make the maple cinnamon ice cream: Prepare the maple ice cream according to the recipe directions. After cooling the base in the ice bath and straining, whisk in the ground cinnamon. Transfer the cooled base to a storage container and refrigerate until ready to use.

2. Make the baked French toast: Preheat the oven to 350°F (175°C). Butter a 12-by-18-inch rimmed baking sheet and line it with parchment paper.

3. In a medium bowl, whisk the eggs until smooth. Add the cream, milk, sugar, 2 teaspoons of the vanilla, and ¼ teaspoon of the cinnamon and whisk to combine. Dip each piece of bread into the egg mixture, flipping the bread to coat all sides and allow it to absorb as much of the egg mixture as possible. Place the coated bread slices on the prepared baking sheet and set aside.

4. In a mixer on medium speed, beat the butter, brown sugar, syrup, remaining 1 teaspoon vanilla, and the remaining ¼ teaspoon cinnamon until combined. Spread evenly over the bread slices. Bake for 20 minutes, or until the brown sugar bubbles up and the French toast turns brown at the edges. Let the toast cool completely and then chop it into bite-size pieces.

5. Transfer the cooled base to an ice cream maker and churn it according to the manufacturer's instructions.

6. Transfer the ice cream to a storage container, folding in the baked French toast pieces as you do. Use as much of the toast as you want; you won't necessarily need the whole batch. Serve immediately or harden in your freezer for 8 to 12 hours for a more scoopable ice cream.

## FOR THE MAPLE CINNAMON ICE CREAM:

1 recipe maple ice cream (see page 75)

1 teaspoon ground cinnamon

## FOR THE BAKED FRENCH TOAST:

Butter for the baking sheet

5 eggs

¾ cup (180 ml) heavy cream

¾ cup (180 ml) milk

½ cup (100 g) organic cane sugar

3 teaspoons vanilla extract

½ teaspoon ground cinnamon

6 thin slices of bread (see Note)

14 tablespoons (210 g) unsalted butter

½ cup (110 g) packed dark brown sugar

2 tablespoons golden syrup

Note: We prefer to use a peasant loaf or a sourdough bread, but feel free to experiment to find your favorite!

# HOW TO DRAW WALT

1. ears

2. NOSE

3. Face!

4. ADD AN EXPRESSION!

5. BACK

6. TAIL!

7. BODY!

8. ADD LEGS!

9. AND COLOR!

10. NOW MAKE HIM DANCE

# THE CREAMY CYCLONE

## CREATED AND NAMED BY FACEBOOK FAN DANI ARONSON

**Deep-fry thermometer**

**Piping bag for funnel cake batter**

### FOR THE POPCORN ICE CREAM:

**2 cups (480 ml) whole milk**

**6 cups (90 g) kettle corn**

**⅔ cup (130 g) organic cane sugar**

**½ cup (60 g) skim milk powder**

**1⅔ cups (400 ml) heavy cream**

**3 egg yolks**

During the long winter months, when sales naturally slow, Brian and his team have more time to get wild in the kitchen. It becomes a sport, a competition of sorts, to see who can come up with the most labor-intensive flavor. The Creamy Cyclone takes the cake, but it's not even one of the crew's ideas! This one came from a fan contest on Facebook. We provided the framework: Come up with a flavor that was an ode to Coney Island and included nuts. (Yes, there were some suggestions that included Nathan's hot dogs, but hot dogs aren't bacon, so forget about it.) As hard as Brian and his team have tried, they haven't come up with a tougher flavor than this one. It captures all the elements of a summer afternoon on the boardwalk: kettle corn–infused ice cream with salted peanuts, ribbons of salted fudge caramel, and oh, yeah, pieces of homemade funnel cake!

1. Make the popcorn ice cream: Prepare an ice bath in the sink or in a large heatproof bowl.

2. In a large saucepan, heat the milk over medium-high heat until it starts to steam, 10 to 15 minutes. Remove the pan from the heat, add the kettle corn, and stir. Cover the pan and let the popcorn steep for 20 minutes. Pour the mixture through a wire-mesh strainer into a bowl, pressing down on the popcorn to extract as much milk as possible. Don't worry if some of the popcorn "pulp" pushes through into the ice cream. That's totally OK. Return the kettle corn–infused milk to the saucepan.

3. Add the sugar and skim milk powder. Stir with a hand mixer or whisk until smooth. Make sure the skim milk powder is wholly dissolved into the mixture and that no lumps remain (any remaining sugar granules will dissolve over the heat). Stir in the cream.

THE CYCLONE CONEY ISLAND, N.Y.
CYCLONE
CYCLONE
CYCLONE

4. Clip a candy thermometer to the saucepan and set the pan over medium heat. Cook, stirring often with a rubber spatula and scraping the bottom of the pan to prevent sticking and burning, until the mixture reaches 110°F (45°C), 5 to 10 minutes. Remove the pan from the heat.

5. Place the egg yolks in a medium bowl. While whisking, slowly pour ½ cup (120 ml) of the hot milk mixture into the egg yolks to temper them. Continue to whisk slowly until the mixture is an even color and consistency, then whisk the egg-yolk mixture back into the remaining milk mixture.

6. Return the pan to the stovetop over medium heat and continue cooking the mixture, stirring often, until it reaches 165°F (75°C), 5 to 10 minutes more.

7. Transfer the pan to the prepared ice bath and let cool for 15 to 20 minutes. Pour the ice cream base through a wire-mesh strainer into a storage container and place in the refrigerator for 1 to 2 hours, or until completely cool.

8. Make the funnel cake: In a deep heavy saucepan, heat 1½ inches (4 cm) of oil until it registers 375°F (190°C) on a deep-fry thermometer.

9. In a medium bowl, whisk together the egg, milk, and vanilla. In a separate medium bowl, whisk together the flour, cane sugar, brown sugar, baking powder, and salt. Add the flour mixture to the egg mixture and whisk to combine.

(continued)

Vegetable oil for deep-frying

1 egg

⅔ cup (160 ml) whole milk

½ teaspoon vanilla extract

1¼ (155 g) cups all-purpose flour

1 tablespoon organic cane sugar

1 tablespoon packed dark brown sugar

1 teaspoon baking powder

¼ teaspoon salt

1 cup (100 g) confectioners' sugar, for dusting

1 recipe salted fudge caramel (see page 120)

½ cup (75 g) roasted salted peanuts

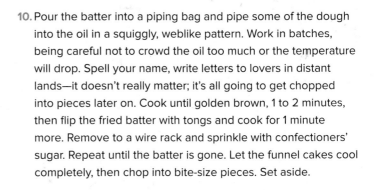

10. Pour the batter into a piping bag and pipe some of the dough into the oil in a squiggly, weblike pattern. Work in batches, being careful not to crowd the oil too much or the temperature will drop. Spell your name, write letters to lovers in distant lands—it doesn't really matter; it's all going to get chopped into pieces later on. Cook until golden brown, 1 to 2 minutes, then flip the fried batter with tongs and cook for 1 minute more. Remove to a wire rack and sprinkle with confectioners' sugar. Repeat until the batter is gone. Let the funnel cakes cool completely, then chop into bite-size pieces. Set aside.

11. Prepare the salted fudge caramel according to the recipe directions.

12. Transfer the cooled base to an ice cream maker and churn it according to the manufacturer's instructions. When the ice cream is almost finished, open the lid and fold in the peanuts and pieces of funnel cake. Use as much of the cake as you want; you won't necessarily need the whole batch. Continue churning for a few minutes more.

13. Transfer the ice cream to a storage container, gently folding in heaping spoonfuls of the salted fudge caramel as you do, softly lifting and spinning it throughout the ice cream. Be careful not to overmix. Serve immediately or harden in your freezer for 8 to 12 hours for a more scoopable ice cream.

# DOUBLE DUTCH LOVE

CREATED AND NAMED BY OUR FACEBOOK FAN
AND LOYAL CUSTOMER ADRIENNE ALMEIDA

The task in this Facebook fan contest was to create a flavor that embodied the three themes of our cookbook: Brooklyn, *Leaves of Grass*, and childhood. The winner would have their flavor made at the shop and included in the cookbook.

Calling Adrienne a loyal customer is an understatement. Adrienne first came into Ample Hills during our first four days when she was nine months pregnant. Her daughter Neva is now over two years old and her first taste of ice cream was Double Dutch Love.

You are not really an Amployee until you've met and been approved by Adrienne. We save her homemade cones, get her thoughts on flavor names, and give her extra servings of hot fudge. And our cookbook would not be complete without her in it.

That being said, Adrienne's entry in the flavor contest was our favorite: corn ice cream with dark chocolate–covered homemade cones.

═══════════ 🍦 ═══════════

1. Make the corn ice cream: Prepare an ice bath in the sink or in a large heatproof bowl.

2. In a large saucepan, heat the milk over medium-high heat until it starts to steam, 10 to 15 minutes. Remove the pan from the heat and stir in the corn. Cover the pan and let the corn steep for 30 minutes. Pour the mixture through a wire-mesh strainer into a bowl, pressing down on the corn to extract as much milk as possible. Don't worry if some of the corn "pulp" pushes through into the ice cream. That's totally OK. Return the corn-infused milk to the saucepan.

3. Add the sugar and skim milk powder. Stir with a hand mixer or whisk until smooth. Make sure the skim milk powder is wholly dissolved into the mixture and that no lumps remain (any remaining sugar granules will dissolve over the heat). Stir in the cream.

(continued)

## FOR THE CORN ICE CREAM:

1¾ cups (420 ml) whole milk

1¾ cups (245 g) organic frozen sweet corn

⅔ cup (130 g) organic cane sugar

½ cup (60 g) skim milk powder

1¾ cups (420 ml) heavy cream

2 egg yolks

## FOR THE CHOCOLATE-COVERED CONES:

1 recipe Ice Cream Cones (page 199)

Butter for the baking sheet

1 pound (455 g) 55% cacao semisweet chocolate

¼ cup (50 g) vegetable shortening

Neva's first ice cream EVER was a scoop of Double Dutch Love!

4. Clip a candy thermometer to the saucepan and set the pan over medium heat. Cook, stirring often with a rubber spatula and scraping the bottom of the pan to prevent sticking and burning, until the mixture reaches 110°F (45°C), 5 to 10 minutes. Remove the pan from the heat.

5. Place the egg yolks in a medium bowl. While whisking, slowly pour ½ cup (120 ml) of the hot milk mixture into the egg yolks to temper them. Continue to whisk slowly until the mixture is an even color and consistency, then whisk the egg-yolk mixture back into the remaining milk mixture.

6. Return the pan to the stovetop over medium heat and continue cooking the mixture, stirring often, until it reaches 165°F (75°C), 5 to 10 minutes more.

7. Transfer the pan to the prepared ice bath and let cool for 15 to 20 minutes, stirring occasionally. Pour the ice cream base through a wire-mesh strainer into a storage container and place in the refrigerator for 1 to 2 hours, or until completely cool.

8. Make the chocolate-covered cones: Prepare as directed, but do not roll them into cone shapes. Lay the flat discs of deliciousness on paper towels to cool. The paper towels will absorb any excess moisture. Making an entire batch of cones will take about 30 minutes or so, but it's a relaxing process and you can snack along the way.

9. Butter a 12-by-18-inch baking sheet and line it with parchment paper.

10. In a small saucepan, combine the chocolate and shortening over low heat, stirring until the chocolate is completely melted and the mixture is smooth.

11. Dip the cone discs, one by one, into the chocolate and coat them completely. Use a spatula to spread the chocolate evenly over each disc. Place the dipped discs in layers on the baking sheet. You should end up with about six stacks of four to five cones each.

12. Cover the baking sheet with aluminum foil and place it in the freezer until the cone layers are firm, about 1 hour. Chop the cones into bite-size pieces. (They'll look a little like Kit Kats with the layers of cone and chocolate.)

13. Transfer the cooled base to an ice cream maker and churn it according to the manufacturer's instructions.

14. Transfer the ice cream to a storage container, folding in the cone pieces as you do. Use as many of the cone pieces as you want; you won't necessarily need the whole batch. Serve immediately or harden in your freezer for 8 to 12 hours for a more scoopable ice cream.

## KIDS' CORNER

We coat the cones in chocolate to protect them from getting soggy in the ice cream. The layered chocolate-covered cones are a fun way to involve your kids. Depending on their ages, they could help you arrange the cones on the baking sheet. Or after the chocolate-covered cones have frozen, have your kids pop them out of the tray and break them into smaller pieces. What do they look like? The striated pieces are a homemade version of a favorite candy bar—Kit Kats!

# BARCLAYS GRIDLOCK

1 recipe brownies (see page 171)

1 recipe coffee ice cream (see page 138)

½ cup (75 g) roasted salted peanuts

¼ cup (45 g) semisweet chocolate chips

1 cup (75 g) chocolate-covered pretzels, chopped

In November 2012, the Barclays Center opened just a few blocks from Ample Hills. We greeted the new arena with excitement, reservations, and an all-out fear of traffic Armageddon. All anyone could talk about leading up to the opening of the center was the impending Jay-Z gridlock. We decided to embrace our conflicting moods with this jam-packed flavor—peanuts, brownies, chocolate chips, and chocolate-covered pretzels in coffee ice cream. Though it was a joke, the combination of flavors proved popular. So we kept making it, even though, to our surprise and joy, Barclays "Car-mageddon" never materialized.

1. Prepare the brownies according to the recipe directions. Let cool, then chop them into bite-size pieces. Freeze until ready to use.

2. Prepare the coffee ice cream according to the recipe directions. Transfer the cooled base to an ice cream maker and churn it according to the manufacturer's instructions.

3. In a small bowl, toss together the peanuts, chocolate chips, pretzels, and brownie pieces and toss to combine.

4. Transfer the ice cream to a storage container, folding in the peanut mixture as you do. Use as much of the peanut mixture as you want; you won't necessarily need the whole batch. Serve immediately or harden in your freezer for 8 to 12 hours for a more scoopable ice cream.

Jam-pack this flavor with whatever you like! Your favorite CANDY BAR? CRACK Cookies? Go CRAZY! Substitute or add even more!

Empire state of Mind

# PLUS ONE

for when you
want to share
with friends

IN THE PARK, tucked under a soaring maple tree, Walt sits alone at
a picnic table. He's waiting for his friends. And boy, is he ready
for them. He's decked out the table with a wild and wonderful
collection of ice cream treats and toppings. Bowls of hot fudge,
caramel, freshly whipped cream, cookie dough pieces,
hand-rolled spiral cones, and more and more. At the
end of the table is an old-fashioned hand-crank
ice cream maker.

Walt bounces on the bench, anxious and excited to see
his friends.

He spots them! "Over here!" Walt yells to Whitty and
PB. He runs up to them and hugs them, and they hug him
back. "Close your eyes, close your eyes! Don't look!"

He leads them to the picnic table. "OK, are you ready? Are you hungry?
Open your eyes!" Whitty and PB open their eyes. PB hops up and down
and squeals with delight. Walt and Whitty laugh and hug and smile.

"It's beautiful, old friend," Whitty says.

PB heads straight for the ice cream maker and turns the handle. "How
does it work?"

"Let me show you!" Walt exclaims. And he does.
They load the machine with a peanut butter ice
cream mixture and pour ice around the canister,
layering it with rock salt.

Then they take turns cranking the ice cream,
talking about their adventure back in time.

When it's done, Walt scoops out ice cream for
his friends, and they craft their own sundaes.
PB uses every single topping that Walt has
prepared. In fact, it's hard to tell if it's still
an ice cream sundae or just a bowl full of toppings.

The three friends sit and enjoy their ice cream together.

When PB finishes, he pauses, turns to his friends and smiles. "Yummy."

Then he looks down into his empty bowl, and says, "More, please."

Walt laughs, and says, "Of course, let's make more. What flavor
should we make next?"

# ICE CREAM CONES
## MAKES ABOUT 12 CONES

1. Halve the vanilla bean and scrape out the seeds; discard the pod. In a small saucepan, add the seeds and the butter. Place over medium heat and stir until the butter is completely melted.

2. In the bowl of a stand mixer fitted with the paddle attachment, combine the sugar, vanilla, salt, and egg whites. Mix on medium speed until well combined and smooth.

3. Add the butter mixture and mix on low speed until combined. Add the flour and mix on medium speed until just combined and smooth.

4. Ladle ¼ cup (60 ml) of the batter onto the waffle cone maker and cook according to the manufacturer's instructions.

5. Remove the cone disc from the waffle cone maker. Place the tip of the dowel about ½ inch (12 mm) from the edge of the disc and tuck the edge of the cone under the tip of the dowel, forming a tight seal. This will be the point of your cone. Use your pinky finger to seal the point while continuing to roll the cone, keeping the disc as tight as possible to the shape of the dowel.

6. Repeat with the remaining batter. Let each cone cool a few moments and enjoy, or store the cones in an airtight container at room temperature for up to 2 days.

We are very proud of our cone maker, as it's not the traditional waffle cone maker you may see at other ice cream shops. It's special. We had the waffle-patterned metal plates replaced with beautifully designed spirals. The mesmerizing spiral pattern coupled with our homemade vanilla-bean cone flavor makes our cones super-delectable.

**SPECIAL EQUIPMENT:**

Waffle cone maker

Cone-shaped dowel

1 vanilla bean

1 cup (240 g) unsalted butter

1 cup (220 g) packed dark brown sugar

1 tablespoon vanilla extract

1 teaspoon salt

1 cup (240 ml) egg whites

1¼ cups (155 g) all-purpose flour

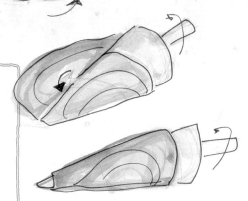

spiral bowls

# HOT FUDGE

MAKES ABOUT 4 CUPS

2 cups (480 ml) heavy cream

1⅔ cups (330 g) organic cane sugar

⅔ cup (160 ml) golden syrup

⅔ cup (60 g) cocoa powder

¼ cup (20 g) whole coffee beans

14 ounces (400 g) semisweet chocolate, chopped

6 tablespoons (90 g) unsalted butter

1 tablespoon vanilla extract

1. In a medium saucepan, combine the cream, sugar, syrup, and cocoa powder and whisk over medium-high heat until well combined. Add the coffee beans. Bring the mixture to a simmer.

2. Add the chocolate and butter and whisk until melted and smooth. Remove the pan from the heat and stir in the vanilla. Pour the hot fudge through a wire-mesh strainer into a bowl to remove the coffee beans. Discard the coffee beans.

3. Serve immediately or store in an airtight container in the refrigerator for up to 2 weeks.

# FROZEN HOT FUDGE

MAKES 2 SERVINGS

1 cup (250 g) Hot Fudge (above), well chilled

⅔ cup (160 ml) whole milk

2 cups ice cubes

Whipped Cream (opposite page), for serving

In a blender, combine the fudge, milk, and ice and blend until the ice is finely chopped and the mixture has a thick, slushy consistency. Serve with a spoon and a dollop of fresh whipped cream on top!

# WHIPPED CREAM

MAKES ABOUT 1½ CUPS

In the bowl of a stand mixer fitted with the whisk attachment, whip the cream, sugar, and vanilla together on high speed until stiff peaks form. Serve immediately or store in the refrigerator for up to 2 hours.

1 cup (240 ml) heavy cream

1 tablespoon organic cane sugar

1 teaspoon vanilla extract

# WET NUTS

MAKES ABOUT 2 CUPS

1. Preheat the oven to 275°F (135°C). Butter a 12-by-18-inch rimmed baking sheet and line it with parchment paper.

2. Spread the walnuts in an even layer on the prepared baking sheet and toast them for 10 to 15 minutes, until fragrant and just starting to brown. Let the walnuts cool, then chop them into small pieces, keeping all the little bits, including the walnut "dust." Set aside.

3. In a medium saucepan, combine the maple syrup, corn syrup, and salt. Cook over medium-high heat until the syrup comes to a boil, then reduce the heat to maintain a simmer and continue to cook for 5 minutes.

4. Remove the pan from the heat and stir in the walnuts (including the walnut dust, which helps flavor the syrup). Add the vanilla and stir to combine. Serve immediately or store in an airtight container in the refrigerator for up to 2 weeks.

Butter for the baking sheet

1 cup (125 g) chopped walnuts

1 cup (240 ml) grade B maple syrup

3 tablespoons corn syrup

Large pinch of salt

1 teaspoon vanilla extract

# SALTED BUTTER
# CARAMEL SAUCE
MAKES ABOUT 2 CUPS

1 cup (200 g) organic cane sugar

2 tablespoons unsalted butter

¾ teaspoon salt

1½ cups (360 ml) heavy cream

½ teaspoon vanilla extract

1. In a medium saucepan, heat the sugar over medium-high heat, stirring frequently with a rubber spatula as it melts. When it has melted completely and drips smoothly off the spatula (with no discernable sugar granules), remove the spatula and continue to cook the sugar without stirring. Watch the pan closely—the caramel will turn darker in color. Watch for smoke to rise off the top. When the caramel starts to smoke, count to ten and remove the pan from the heat.

2. Using an oven mitt, carefully add the butter to the pan. It might spatter when it hits the hot caramel, so be careful. Stir the mixture with a rubber spatula until the butter has melted and the mixture is smooth. Stir in the salt. Slowly pour in the cream—it will bubble up, but you must continue to stir it as you pour, so the cream incorporates smoothly into the caramel. Be careful!

3. Remove the pan from the heat; add the vanilla and stir to combine.

4. Let cool a little before serving, or store the caramel sauce in an airtight container in the refrigerator for up to 2 weeks. (The butter might start to separate, but if you reheat it, you can whisk it until the mixture is combined again.)

# WHISKEY BUTTERSCOTCH

MAKES ABOUT 2 CUPS

1. In a medium saucepan, combine the brown sugar, syrup, butter, and ¼ cup (60 ml) water. Clip a candy thermometer to the saucepan and set the pan over medium-high heat. Cook until the mixture reaches 245°F (118°C).

2. Add the cream and stir to combine, being careful not to let the hot syrup spatter on you. Halve the vanilla bean and scrape out the seeds. Add the seeds and pod, the whisky, and the salt to the pan and cook for 5 minutes more.

3. Remove the pan from the heat and let cool for 10 minutes. Use a fork to remove and discard the vanilla bean pod. Add the vanilla extract and stir to combine.

4. Serve immediately or store in an airtight container in the refrigerator for up to 2 weeks. (The sugar may start to crystallize, but if you reheat it, you can stir until the sugar crystals dissolve.)

1½ cups (330 g) packed dark brown sugar

¼ cup (60 ml) golden syrup

½ cup (120 g) unsalted butter

½ cup (120 ml) heavy cream

1 vanilla bean

¼ cup (60 ml) whisky

¾ teaspoon salt

1 teaspoon vanilla extract

# MARSHMALLOW FLUFF
## MAKES ABOUT 3 CUPS

6 tablespoons (90 ml) pasteurized egg whites

¼ teaspoon cream of tartar

¾ cup (150 g) organic cane sugar

½ cup (120 ml) corn syrup

¼ teaspoon salt

1 vanilla bean

2 teaspoons vanilla extract

1. In the bowl of a stand mixer, combine the egg whites and cream of tartar. Set aside.

2. In a small saucepan, combine the sugar, corn syrup, salt and ¼ cup (60 ml) water and stir.

3. Halve the vanilla bean lengthwise and scrape out the seeds. Add the seeds and pod to the saucepan. Clip a candy thermometer to the side of the pan and set the pan over medium heat.

4. Meanwhile, begin beating the egg-white mixture on high speed, until stiff peaks form.

5. When the sugar mixture reaches 240°F (115°C), remove the pan from the heat. Using a fork, remove and discard the vanilla bean pod.

6. Reduce the mixer speed to low and slowly drizzle the hot sugar syrup in a steady stream into the egg whites. Add the vanilla and raise the mixer speed to high. Whip the mixture until it becomes fluffy, 10 to 12 minutes. Continue whipping until the marshmallow fluff holds its shape.

7. Serve immediately or store in an airtight container in the refrigerator for up to 1 week.

# HOT CHOCOLATE

## MAKES 2 SERVINGS

1. In a medium saucepan, combine the milk, sugar, cocoa powder, salt, and cinnamon. Whisk vigorously until smooth. Cook over medium heat until steaming.

2. Add the chocolates and whisk until melted and smooth. Add the vanilla and whisk until combined.

3. Remove the pan from the heat and serve the hot chocolate immediately, with a dollop of freshly whipped cream on top.

2 cups (480 ml) whole milk

2 tablespoons organic cane sugar

3 tablespoons plus 1 teaspoon cocoa powder

Pinch of salt

⅛ teaspoon ground cinnamon

3 ounces (85 g) milk chocolate, chopped

4 ounces (115 g) semisweet chocolate, chopped

½ teaspoon vanilla extract

Whipped Cream (page 203), for serving

# BUILD YOUR OWN SUNDAE

Each sundae ordered at the shop is unique and made to order, but the ingredients listed here are perfect for birthday parties or even more formal occasions. Take these guidelines and make them your own!

1. Warm a homemade treat of your choice—a brownie, blondie, ooey gooey cake, monkey bread . . . the possibilities are endless. At the shop, we store our portioned homemade treats in the refrigerator (they will keep for up to 1 week, but never last half that long) and warm them in the microwave for 45 seconds when they are ordered.

2. Add a scoop of your favorite ice cream, then add hot caramel or fudge and top with whipped cream and sprinkles (or anything, really—our favorite is crushed crack cookies!).

It's all about layering warm and cold ingredients to create a perfect balance of flavors and temperatures. Once, we created a specialty sundae because we had some extra candied bacon and couldn't bear to let it go to waste. Piggies by the Campfire was a warmed brownie with Gather 'Round the Campfire ice cream (page 60), hot fudge, candied bacon, and a toasted marshmallow on top. (We bought a crème brûlée torch for the occasion and toasted the marshmallows to perfection!)

# BUILD YOUR OWN FLOAT

1 generous scoop ice cream

12 fluid ounces (360 ml) soda

Whipped Cream (page 203) for serving

---

We once made a cotton candy ice cream and orange soda float. Perhaps not for the most sophisticated palette, but the six-year-old who ordered it was certainly very happy!

---

At the shop, we keep a variety of sodas on hand and encourage customers to get creative with the combinations. We have more than fifteen different soda and twenty-four flavors of ice cream! Our favorite combinations at the shop are the Honey Cow (cream soda with Sweet as Honey ice cream, page 44) and the Blushing Cow (cola with Strawberries and Cream, page 50), but there's not anything quite like an old-fashioned Root Beer Float with Vanilla Bean ice cream (page 35).

1.  Slowly pour your soda of choice into a cup. The trick is to pour the soda like you would a beer, down the side of the glass; you want to minimize the foam.

2.  Gingerly place the ice cream into the soda. This is a delicate process—you don't want the soda to explode in your face or all over the counter.

3.  Top with whipped cream and enjoy!

BROOKLY

# CROSSING BROOKLYN FERRY

Our most decadent concoction to date, this epic sundae is our take on a banana split and is recommended for groups of hungry people. It's also completely customizable. You can pick any homemade treat, not just a brownie, and any flavors of ice cream.

1. Warm the brownie for 45 seconds in the microwave.

2. Peel and halve a banana lengthwise and prop it against the sides of a serving dish.

3. Place the three scoops of ice cream in the dish.

4. Layer the hot fudge, caramel sauce, and wet nuts—in your preferred amounts—over the ice cream. Add the whipped cream and sprinkles. And finally, top with a cherry, of course!

1 brownie (see page 171)

1 banana

1 scoop Vanilla Bean (page 34)

1 scoop Dark Chocolate (page 36)

1 scoop Strawberries and Cream (page 50)

Hot Fudge (page 202), to taste

Salted Butter Caramel Sauce (page 204), to taste

Wet Nuts (page 203), to taste

Whipped Cream (page 203), to taste

Sprinkles

1 maraschino cherry

# ICE CREAM CAKE

**SPECIAL EQUIPMENT:**

Silicone mold

8 ounces (225 g) brownie
(see page 171)

6 tablespoons (90 ml) Hot
Fudge (page 202)

3 cups (about 600 g)
Peppermint Pattie (page 151)

3 cups (about 600 g)
Strawberries and Cream
(page 50)

¼ cup (15 g) Whipped Cream
(page 203)

Sprinkles

At Ample Hills, we can
make as many as twenty
cakes a week. They are
one of our most versa-
tile creations—top with
sprinkles and serve at
a birthday party, replace
the base with maca-
roons for Passover, or
ice the cake completely
for a formal wedding—
we've done it all.

You know the best part about ice cream cake? The ice cream!
And in an Ample Hills cake, ice cream is the star ingredient.
We use silicone molds to build our five-layer cakes. Brownies
work best as the bottom layer, but you could use ooey gooey
cake or blondies, too.

The small cake pictured at right was made with a 6-inch
(15-cm) round silicone cake mold. Its six layers are made of the
ingredients listed to the left, but you can substitute other ice cream
flavors, sauces, and baked treats.

1. To assemble the ice cream cake, mush the brownies into the
   base of the mold, forming a layer about as thick as a quarter.
   This layer is mostly for structure, as it provides support for the
   cake once it comes out of the mold.

2. Smooth 3 tablespoons of the fudge on top of the brownie layer,
   then freeze until solid (about 1 hour). Cover the fudge layer
   with a 1-inch (2.5-cm) layer of Peppermint Pattie and freeze until
   solid (about 1 hour). Add another thin layer of fudge and freeze
   again. Add a layer of Strawberries and Cream almost to the top
   of the mold (it's important to leave a small gap at the top of the
   mold for the whipped cream) and freeze overnight.

3. Spoon whipped cream on top of the cake and use a spatula
   to smooth it into a completely level surface. Add sprinkles!

4. Freeze the cake until the whipped cream hardens (about
   1 hour), then gently pop the cake out of the mold and serve.

# ICE CREAM PARTIES!

Having two young children of their own, Brian and Jackie had been to numerous kids' birthday parties. They knew what they liked and they knew what their kids liked. Interactive, creative experiences were paramount. So they brainstormed a way to have kids create their own ice cream in the form of a hand-cranked ice cream maker attached to a bicycle. They worked with a bicycle designer to create the first ever pedal-powered ice cream maker. When the bicycle is not in use, it sits in the window of the shop and beckons kids—and kids at heart—to take a spin. The best part happens when revelers get to devour their creation, smothered with sundae toppings, on top of a homemade waffle.

PIN THE SCOOP

Making it is almost as fun as eating it!

# RESOURCES

### BEANILLA
A great source for vanilla beans and vanilla extracts
**beanilla.com**

### CHEF'S CHOICE WAFFLECONE EXPRESS
Available from **Williams-Sonoma**, **Bed Bath & Beyond**, and
**Amazon.com**

### COUNTRY FREEZER
Old-fashioned hand-crank ice cream makers
**country-freezer.com**

### E. GUITTARD CHOCOLATE
American-made all-natural baking chocolate
**guittard-online.stores.yahoo.net**

### FRONTIER
Assorted all-natural and organic extracts and flavorings
**frontiercoop.com**

### GLEE GUM
All-natural chicle bubble gum
**gleegum.com**

### HOMEMADE SODA COMPANY
Root beer and other flavors for making soda at home
**homemadesodacompany.com**

### MADECASSE
Chocolate and vanilla grown and made in Africa
**madecasse.com**

### NATURE'S FLAVORS
Assorted all-natural and organic flavorings and food colorings
**naturesflavors.com**

# INDEX

# THANK YOU!

## BRIAN

To **Lauren**, without whom this book wouldn't exist. Your passion and your art make the shop a better place. And you know all the right buttons to push, to make me a better boss. To **Nonna** and **Kaleo**. You inspire me. And whenever I'm feeling down, or tired, or scared, you are there to let me see the shop through your wonder-filled eyes. To **Eric**, our GM. Thank you for putting out all the fires. To **Christian** and **Adam**, the dynamic duo. You make coming to work fun. Here's to the never-ending search for the perfect flavor! To the whole staff, for smiling, laughing, and being the most beloved staff in all of Brooklyn! A special thanks to **Chae**, **Eric**, **Jamie**, **Jason**, and **Jenny** for testing recipes. This cookbook wouldn't be delicious without you. To **Rob** at Sullivan County Farms, for supplying us with the best milk, cream, and eggs possible on the East Coast. To **Robb S.**, who helped us launch Ample Hills in a dingy basement, making ice cream pops by hand for hours at a time, volunteering his time because . . . well, just because. Free ice cream for life! **Hege** and **Phyllis**, thank you for your creativity, love, and support. To **Mom**, for flying to New York at a moment's notice when we ran out of ice cream at the beginning and I couldn't see past the next day, let alone the next week. You saved us, and you washed a lot of dishes. Thank you. To **Dad** for supporting me, advising me, and knowing when to back off and let me make my own mistakes. To my beautiful **Jackie**. You believed in me— and pushed me—when I wasn't sure I believed in me. And through some trick of magic, or love, you made Ample Hills a second home for all of us, employees and customers alike. It's your turn now, baby. What are you going to do? Into the mystic. I got you too.

## JACKIE

To all the **moms** who witnessed our struggles of raising a family and starting a business. Thanks for the support. To our most awesome landlords, **Dan** and **Catherine Noble**. Thank you for choosing us and not Chase Bank. Your entire community is grateful! To **Phebe** and **Ohad**, who were there from the beginning. Thank you for living two doors down from our shop and making us spectacular dinners. I'm happy we can always provide dessert! To **Debbie**. Thank you for being my right-hand event scooper at a moment's notice. We make a great team! Thank you to **Danielle Galland** for designing our space into the warm, beautiful shop it is. Thank you **Lucy** for the gorgeous photos. Thank you to the most intelligent and talented **staff** any shop could have. We only wish we could keep you forever. To **Lauren**, who immediately got our vibe. It takes a special someone. And thank you for always being a positive and inspirational energy throughout the shop. Thanks, **Dad**, for your heartfelt songs and stories to our kids. Your creativity has infected us all and for that I am grateful. To **Mom**, whose passion for good food and community will forever inspire me. My understanding and love for you only get stronger as I continue to miss you immensely. To **Nonna** and **Kaleo** for being so yummy! I love watching you grow and change and be who you are. To my **Brian**, whose never-ending love and compassion warm my heart and feed my soul every single day. Thank you for thinking big while somehow managing to be the most present father and loving husband I have ever seen. You are truly amazing!

## LAUREN

**Jackie** and **Brian**, thank you for being my bosses and friends, and letting me cover your store with doodles of pigs. You value the talent and individuality of your employees and it makes your business and community more colorful for it. To my fellow **Amployees**, past and present. Your propeller hats, rotating playlists, and positive attitudes make Ample Hills what it is and this cookbook wouldn't be complete without you. To **Laura**, **Danielle**, and the whole Abrams team, and to **Kari**, our wonderful agent. Thank you for making this book a reality. To **Walt**, **Whitty**, and especially **PB**. You are chunky and adorable. To the **kids** who know these characters by name. To **my family**, who are ceaselessly supportive of my winding career path. And to **Jen**: the silliest goose.

Published in 2014 by ABRAMS

Text copyright © 2014 Brian Smith and Jackie Cuscuna
Illustrations copyright © 2014 Lauren Kaelin
Photographs copyright © 2014 Lucy Schaeffer

Library of Congress Control Number: 2013945634

ISBN: 978-1-61769-076-1

Editor: Laura Dozier
Designer: Danielle Young
Production Manager: True Sims

The text of this book was composed in Aracne and Proxima Nova.

Printed and bound in the U.S.A.

10 9 8 7 6

ABRAMS books are available at special discounts when
purchased in quantity for premiums and promotions as well as fundraising
or educational use. Special editions can also be created to specification.
For details, contact specialsales@abramsbooks.com or the address below.

ABRAMS The Art of Books
195 Broadway, New York, NY 10007
abramsbooks.com

FROLIC ON,
CRESTED & scallop-edg'd
waves!

gorgeous clouds
of the
SUN-SET!

drench with your
splendor
me,
OR THE MEN
&
women
generations after
me.

Ebinger's

CROSS FROM SHORE TO SHORE,
countless crowds of passengers!
Stand up, tall masts of Mannahatta!—
Stand up, beautiful hills of Brooklyn!
Throb, baffled and curious brain!
throw out questions & answers!